Melissa Leapman

color knitting

Essential Techniques,
Perfect Palettes,
and Fresh Designs
Using Just One Color
at at Time

the easy way

POTTER
CRAFT

NEW YORK

Contents

How to Use this Book

Walk into any yarn shop

and you'll discover every **color** of the rainbow on display, from cool blues and liquid greens to spicy reds and shimmering golds; from crisp, bright white to the soft hues of cream, sand, and ecru—and more shades of purple than could ever be knit in a lifetime.

For many knitters, though, the tantalizing array of beautifully colored yarns can be at once inspiring and overwhelming. Students in my workshops often ask me, "How do I choose **colors** that work well together?" It's a question quickly followed by, "What **colors** will coordinate nicely with leftover yarn from my stash?" For these knitters, Chapter 1 explores basic color theory, including information specific to the needs of knitters as yarn lovers: selecting, combining, and substituting colors. And, you'll find complete **color** guides for every combination around the color wheel for quick reference no matter what project you are choosing yarn for. Have a three-**color** pattern you're just dying to try? Flip to my Three-**Color** Combinations guide (page 14) and choose your favorite for a project with guaranteed designer style. Guided by a few basic principles, anyone can devise **color** palettes suited to any project, occasion, and person on his or her knitting list.

Of course, when I talk about getting started with **color** knitting, many people simply respond with a reflexive *"But isn't multicolor knitting difficult?"* Happily, I answer this last question with a resounding "Absolutely not!" All knitters—whether beginning or advanced, occasional hobbyists or dedicated, daily knitters—can confidently create beautiful colorways for their projects and easily, successfully knit them. In this book we'll explore two of the easiest and most popular ways of knitting with multiple **colors**, using just one **color** at a time.

One-color, one-row stitch techniques allow for a minimal learning curve but yield maximum impact. In the pages that follow, we'll tackle key techniques, explore infinite design possibilities, and knit projects to hone our skills along the way.

Of all one-color, one-row **color**-knitting techniques, stripes may be the most ubiquitous, and for good reason. Easy, versatile, and fun to knit, stripes offer the perfect introduction to knitting with **color**. If you are new to **color** knitting or are looking for a refresher course, you will want to start here to learn all the basics, such as starting and ending a new yarn, knitting multiple colors in the round, and weaving in yarn tails like a pro. Even those with color knitting experience will find tips and tricks to make their projects quicker and easier to knit using as many yarns as they can imagine. Stripes may seem simple, but with an educated choice of **color** combinations, interesting fabrics can result—even in humble stockinette stitch. Add some texture, and stripes can be showy and positively breathtaking! A few garter stitch ridges add depth; tuck stitches, formed by working into stitches several rows below the active row, make unusual puckered fabrics. Strategically placed increases and decreases create beautiful ripple patterns.

Other popular color-knitting techniques such as slip stitch and mosaic knitting also use only one **color** per row, yielding fabrics that are easier to knit than they appear. Pulling up stitches up from a previous row creates *the illusion* of intricacy without much effort. With these slip stitch techniques, an infinite number of graphic shapes and designs can be knitted in, including Greek keys and tongue-and-groove patterns.

Projects in each chapter will put key color knitting techniques into practice and treasuries of **color** patterns for both striped and slip stitch designs will keep your needles knitting in all the **colors** of the rainbow for years to come. With this collection of beautiful, colorful stitch patterns, you can easily adapt any project to your unique taste and style—in more than 60 different ways! Use the **color**-coded page ends to help you easily find just the project or pattern you are looking for.

In addition, a useful how-to section in the back of the book includes basic instructions for chart reading, general knitting and finishing techniques, and using the pattern treasuries. It'll be your go-to spot if any unfamiliar term or abbreviation comes up, and the resources there will help to ensure your knitting success—and enjoyment—now and in the future.

We've got lots of great material to explore together. Let's begin...

Understanding Color

Orange, green, yellow, blue, violet, red—even red-violet and more! With today's yarns available in so many delectable colors, it's not surprising that many knitters find the whole idea of color—from selecting to combining to substituting—a little intimidating.

And no wonder! The entire system of color theory was developed by none other than Sir Isaac Newton in the late seventeenth century. (Finally, my years as a premed student studying physics have paid off.) Newton used a prism to separate clear light into the spectrum of colors and arranged the colors in a circle that we call the color wheel. The relationship of colors around the circumference of that circle comprises color theory, as we'll explore in this chapter.

Any artist—or modern fashionista, for that matter—will tell you that color is not merely a scientific attribute. The writer Johann Goethe, in fact, explored the psychological effects of color in his *Zür Farbenlehre* [*Theory of Color*] in 1820. He believed that our perception of color affected the "sensation" of it. And I would have to agree with him. Even armed with all my undergraduate years of science, I still find that color remains a subjective experience. If you don't believe me, just ask any five-year-old who refuses to wear anything but her orange floral T-shirt with her purple printed skirt today (and possibly tomorrow, too). So, just as no one needs a book on music

theory—let alone a stodgy music critic—to tell him or her what kind of music to enjoy, no one should rely completely on the conventions of color theory to describe the only—or even the best—ways to use color. Yet color theory can be a powerful tool for knitters. Whether it serves as a starting point, a rule book, or a saving grace, the following material can guide us toward educated color choices. As you experiment with color, its varied combinations, and its relationship to yarn, keep in mind that like most things in life, the best part of art and creative design often comes from the unexpected.

Above: The color wheel shows relationships among hues.

Talking About Color
Of course, knowing about Isaac Newton's prismatic experience may make you a much-coveted partner in science trivia games, but it won't mean much for your knitting unless you can put the color wheel into practice. To do that you'll want to be able to describe color using some key terms: hue, value, and saturation.

Hue describes what we normally think of as "color," straight out of a crayon box: red, green, blue, or yellow-orange, for example. For our purposes here, a hue refers to a color family, a specific spot on the color wheel. The color wheel shows the relationship between hues, and the primary colors (red, yellow, and blue) form its foundation. Together, these three hues create every other color in the spectrum. Their opposites across the wheel (green, violet, and orange) are the secondary colors. Combine a primary with its neighboring secondary color and you'll create a tertiary color that falls between the two. So, red and orange will create red-orange and so forth.

If this takes you back to grade school, bear with me; understanding the relationship between primary, secondary, and tertiary colors becomes important when selecting color palettes for your knitting. Certain hues are considered "warm"—reds, oranges, and yellows. Other colors are "cool"—violets, blues, and greens. These "temperatures" describe a color's undertone, and you can use this knowledge to your design advantage. You can make a palette feel cohesive by choosing colors with the same temperature or add a single color from the opposite temperature to make a pattern "pop." Warm colors tend to advance visually in a design, while cool colors seem to recede. Many sweater designers use this illusion to cleverly distract the eye from a wearer's figure flaws while highlighting other areas with a decorative yoke or a neckline, for example.

Value refers to the relative lightness or darkness of a hue on a gray scale (which shows all the possible shades of gray from black through white), but for our purposes it can be used to talk about the amount of contrast between two colors. Because we typically analyze yarn by hue, it may take some practice to learn how to evaluate yarn according to its value as well. However, value plays an important role in colorwork. The greater the contrast between yarn values in a palette, the sharper and crisper the stitch pattern will be. This is clearly no small consideration when working an intricate stitch!

Below: The cool colors on the color wheel tend to visually recede while the warm colors advance.

A color's technical value on the gray scale is constant; however, its perceived value is not and depends on its juxtaposition with other colors in a particular pattern or design. For example, a Caribbean blue might seem dark within a pastel palette; the same color could appear light and bright when placed next to a darker color such as navy. To compare the values of several colors, use a digital camera, computer scanner, or photocopier to create a grayscale image of colors side by side. As you become more adept at judging value, you'll quickly be able to evaluate yarns on their own. A handy shortcut is to place a sheet of transparent red plastic (often available at quilting stores) over the colors you'd like to knit

with. The red plastic acts as a filter and enables you to see the comparative values of the yarn.

Saturation describes the relative pureness of a color and is determined by the amount of white, gray, or black that's been added. Highly saturated colors are bright; those with lower saturations appear duller. Adding white to a pure color lightens its saturation and creates a **tint**, adding gray muddies its saturation and creates a **tone**, and adding black deepens its saturation and creates a **shade**. A combination of shades, tones, and tints creates a nearly infinite assortment of harmonious color palettes for knitted projects—all based upon just one hue, or color family. This combination is called monochromatic.

Selecting and Combining Colors When selecting and combining colors, we aim to achieve color harmony—a balance of colors that neither bores nor overexcites the eye. The following six groups of color combinations will give you a place to start, whether you plan to select an additional color (or colors) to coordinate with a specific yarn or develop an entire color palette from scratch. For us as knitters, the mechanics of color theory are less important than discovering which color combinations work well together, so let's get started!

Monochromatic Color Combinations

Monochromatic colorways use only colors of the same hue and may be comprised of tints, tones, and shades. In this sort of color story, choose a hue based on what temperature you wish your final color palette to have. Warm-color families, such as red, produce energizing and exciting monochromatic combinations, while various shades and tints of a cool-color family, such as blue, will create a soothing palette.

Although monochromatic combinations limit the hues in a color palette, they certainly do not limit opportunities for creativity. When working with a monochromatic palette, there are many ways to change colors throughout your knitted design. You may choose to subtly shift from the lightest color to the darkest and then reverse the colors, moving from dark to light. Or you may want to deliberately shock the eye by placing the darkest color next to the lightest color for sharp contrast.

Monochromatic combinations often project a timeless, classic quality, making them ideal for home decor items and for sophisticated menswear.

Two-Color Combinations

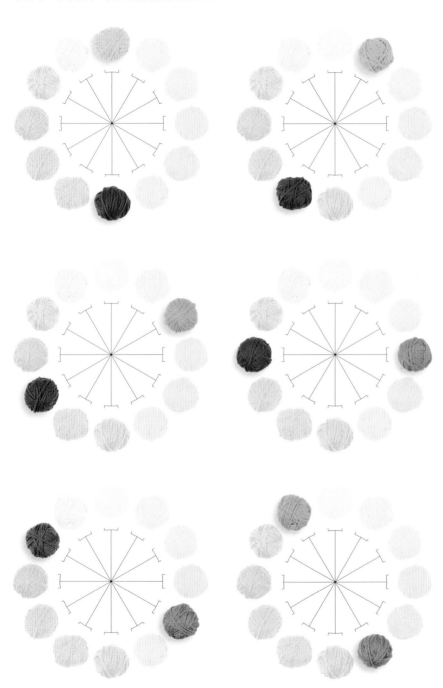

Complementary Colors

Colors directly opposite each other on the color wheel are called complementary colors. This type of combination creates dramatic visual effects, even when the colors are used as tints or shades, because they contrast sharply in hue and temperature. Christmas red and green, for instance, are beautifully matched complements. For reference, here are all six of the complementary combinations on the color wheel.

Two-Color Combinations

Counterpoint Colors

This combination teams up one color with a color on either side of its complement across the color wheel. The two hues used in the Op Art Wine Cozy (page 134) are counterpoints, for example. Here are all twelve of the counterpoint color groupings on the color wheel.

Counterpoint colors, used less frequently than complementary combinations, add a modern and fresh look to designs. Many designers use counterpoint colors for trendy home decor projects and for striking wardrobe accents.

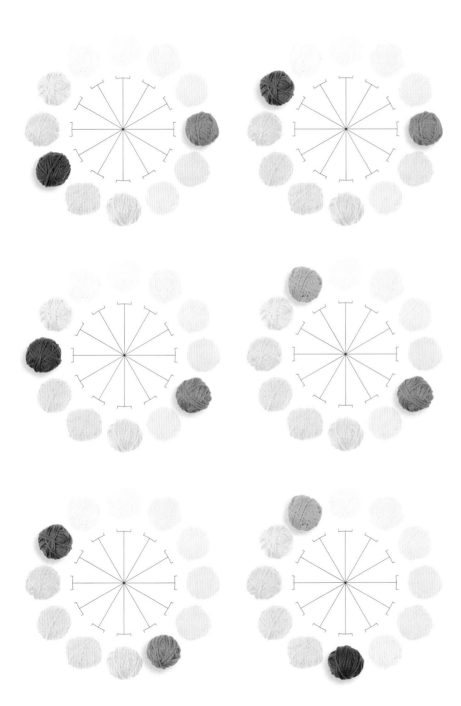

Three-Color Combinations

Triad Colors

For a balanced color story, choose a set of triads. This combination consists of three hues that are evenly spaced apart on the color wheel. For example, the three primary colors (yellow, red, and blue) make up one triad, and the three secondary colors (orange, violet, and green) comprise another. Here's what all four triad combinations look like.

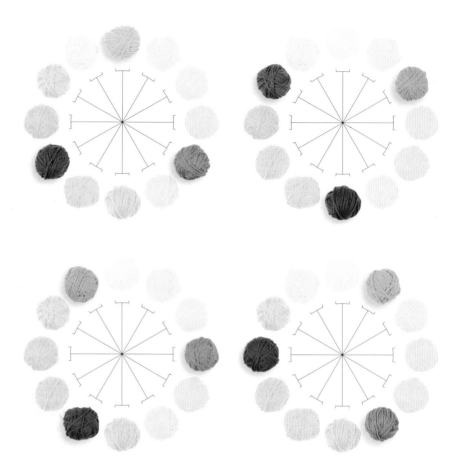

color **PLAY**

Keep a color journal or create an inspiration board to develop your sense for color. Fill it with clippings that reflect color combinations you love. You might include photographs, advertisements, bits of yarn, paint chips, pictures from catalogs—anything that catches your eye.

Left: A three-color analogous
color combination creates a
sense of playfulness in April's
Sweater Dress (page 128).

Three-Color Combinations

Split Complementary Colors

Split complementary combinations are made up of one color plus the colors on both sides of its complement. Although similar to the two-color complementary colorway, this grouping of colors often yields a fresher-looking pal-ette than one that utilizes only a direct complement. It's suitable for sophisti-cated projects.

The direct complement to yellow, for example, is violet, so the com-ponents of a three-color split complementary colorway with yellow are blue-violet and red-violet. Here are all twelve pos-sible split complementary color combinations on the color wheel.

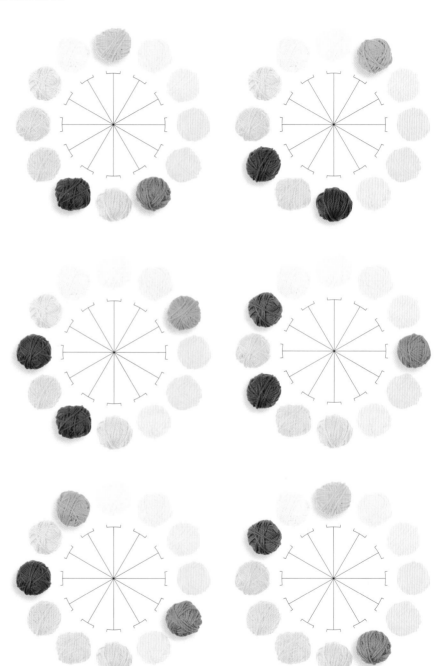

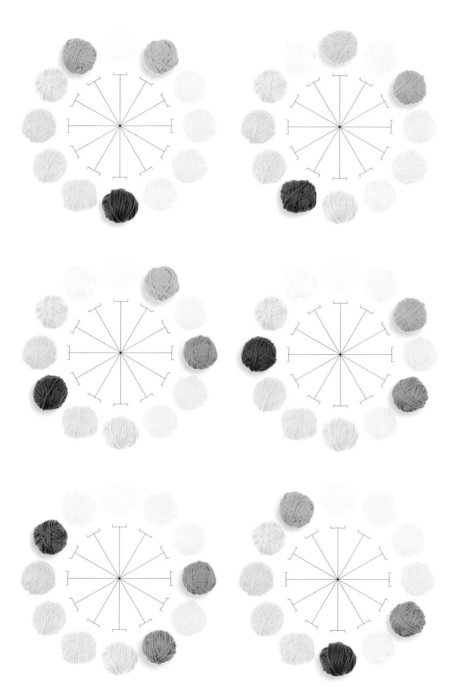

color **PLAY**

As I travel the country to teach workshops, I'm often asked how to create a beautiful colorway that uses a yarn that's languishing in the stash. My advice: Get out a color wheel, find that color's complement, and add the two colors on either side of it to create a split complementary combo.

Three-Color Combinations

Analogous Colors

Analogous color combinations consist of three colors adjacent to one another on the color wheel. Imagine a child's sweater knitted in red, red-orange, and orange: Although visually exciting, the grouping is as harmonious as a man's skully worked in blue-violet, blue, and blue-green. Because they're close in temperature, analogous colors are particularly compatible and create more depth than simple monochromatic ones. April's Sweater Dress (page 128) is an example of an analogous colorway. Here are all twelve of the analogous color combinations on the color wheel.

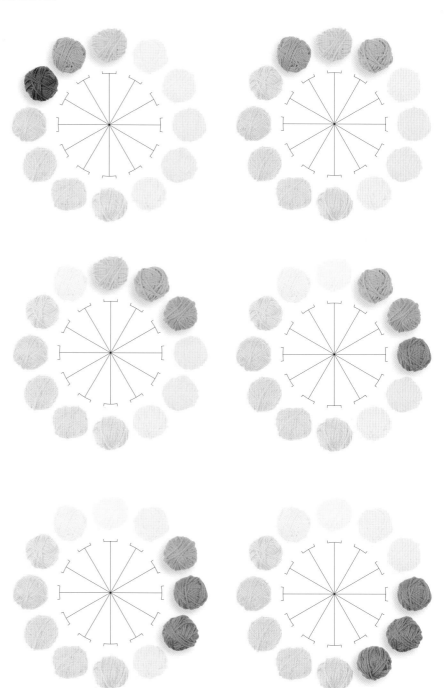

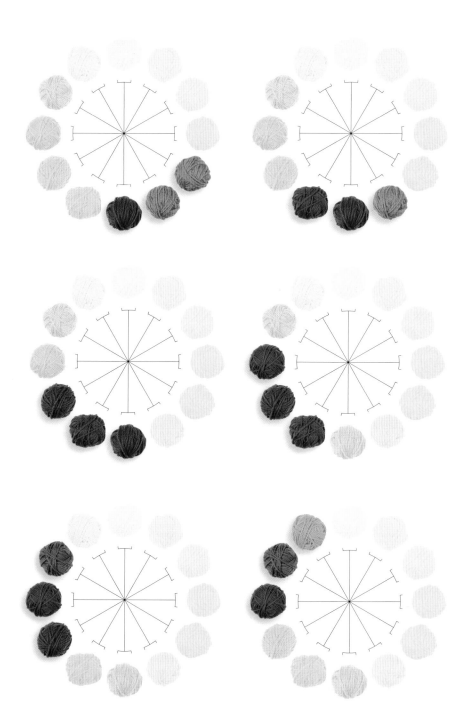

Four-Color Combinations

Square Tetrad Colors

Two pairs of complementary colors that create a square shape on the color wheel comprise square tetrad colors. Here, each of the four colors is equidistant from the others, creating tension—and interest—in the combination. Following are the three possible square tetrad colorways.

 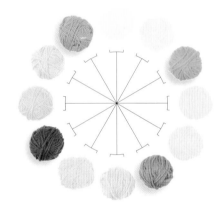

Everyday Inspirations

Great color palettes don't just come off of a color wheel, of course. Even if you never study the physics or psychology of color theory, you can create beautiful color combinations simply by looking at the world around you.

For tried-and-true combinations, use the colorways you see every day in nature. Perhaps you are inspired by the blues and greens of the ocean. Or you might love the colors of sunset: midnight blue with red-violet, both mixed with orange. Do you enjoy hiking in the mountains, or do you prefer the high deserts of the American West? Each environment offers completely different palettes to inspire you.

Of course, there's more than just the natural world to draw upon for ideas. If you're a history buff, you might be excited by the clothing and art from a particular period. A stroll through a museum offers myriad color combinations, from antique quilts to unique styles (and colors) of dress in the Chinese dynasties to a favorite era in art history. Collect postcards of paintings or pieces you particularly love or bring a sketchbook with you and take notes on things you find exhilarating. It's amazing how, even many years later, these mementos can provide creative inspiration!

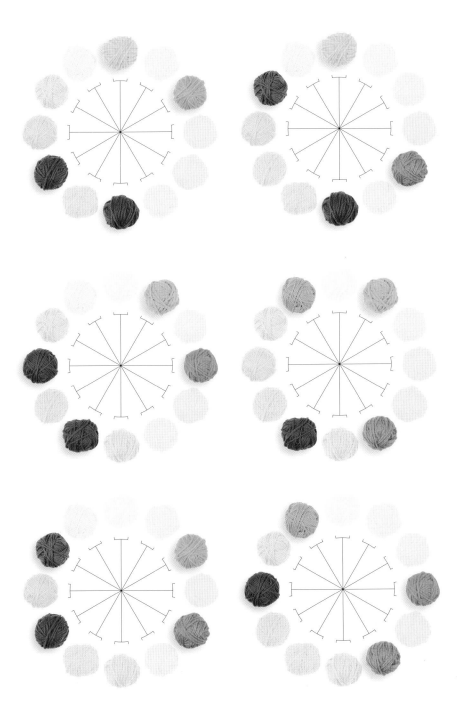

Rectangular Tetrad Colors

Two pairs of complementary colors that create a rect-angular shape on the color wheel comprise rectangular tetrads. This type of color-way is ideal for designs for teens and tweens and for any project in which lots of eye movement and attention is desired. Here are all six possible combinations on the color wheel.

Four-Color Combinations

Analogous Colors with a Complement

Here, a group of three adjacent colors on the color wheel are teamed up with the complementary color directly opposite them. The addition of the comple-ment offers an unexpected blast of energy and edge to a design. Striped Finger-less Mitts (page 62) utilize this type of colorway plus navy. Try this sort of color combination in your next project, using just a touch of the complement with equal amounts of each of the analogous colors. You'll feel like a color genius! Here are all twelve possible combina-tions on the color wheel.

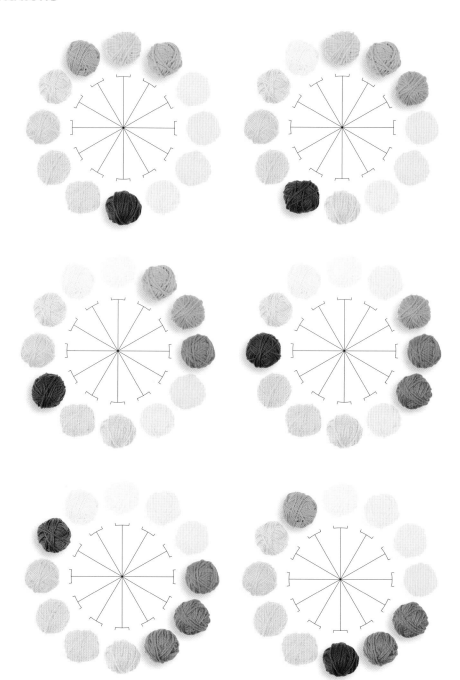

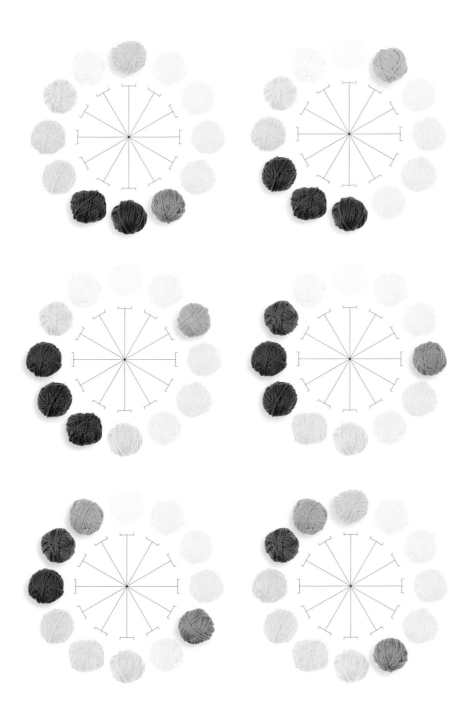

Four-Color Combinations

Double Complementary Colors

This harmonious type of colorway combines two adjacent colors on the color wheel with both of their direct complements. The use of complements in these combinations creates lots of eye movement in the palettes. The result is often energetic yet sophisticated. Here are all six possibilities on the color wheel.

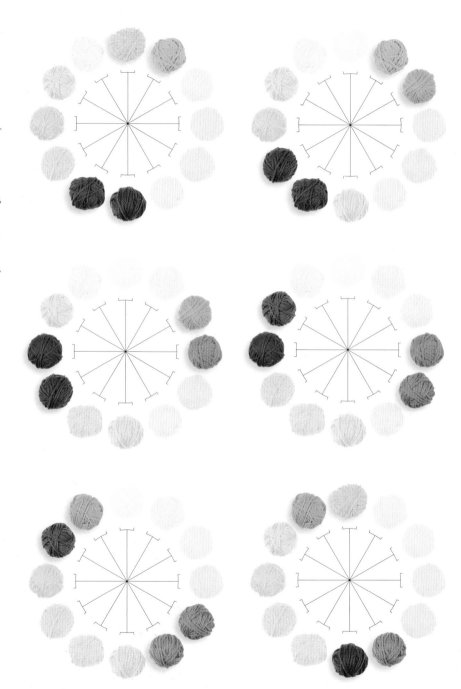

Left: These Striped Fingerless Mitts (page 62) feature a rich four-color "analogous with a complement" colorway.

Five-Color Combinations

Double Split Complementary Colors

The twelve double split complementary combinations offer a wealth of design possibilities. Simply choose one color and add the two colors on each side of the hue's complement. The balance of the two colors nearly opposite on the color wheel adds tension to the palette as well as a certain edgy quality, making these colorways great for playful kid's stuff and fun, trendy women's wear. Here are the twelve possible double split complementary combinations on the color wheel.

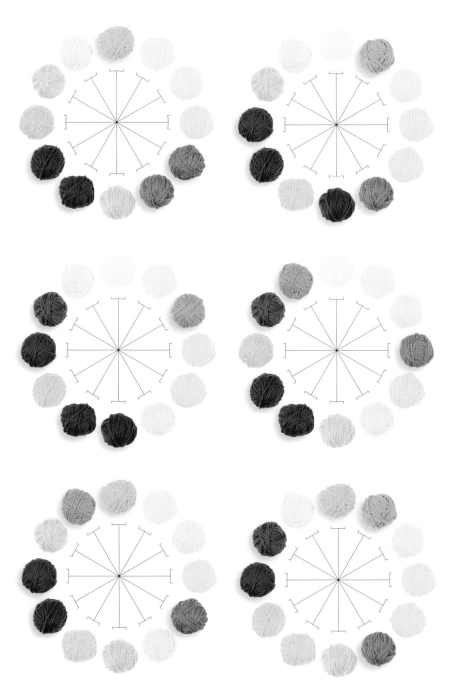

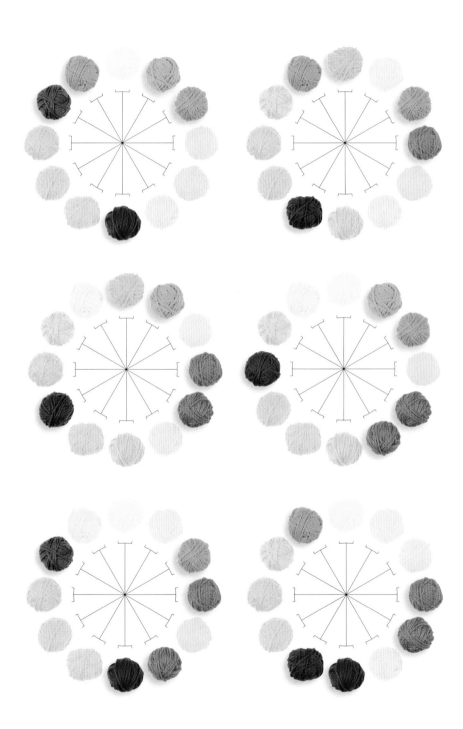

Six-Color Combinations

Double Triad Colors

This grouping of colors consists of two sets of triads, one adjacent to the other. With so much variety in hue, these combinations are lots of fun to play with. Try using a lighter tint of one triad with a darker tint of the other. Or, for more subtlety, allow one pair of adjacent colors to dominate, while using the other colors in smaller amounts for pattern contrast. Here are the four possible combinations.

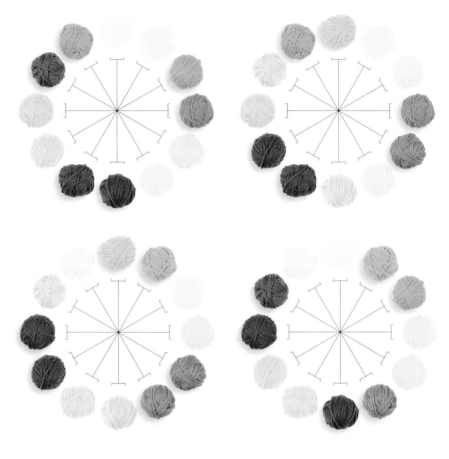

Hexad Colors

This combination is made up of every other color on the color wheel: three pairs of complementary colors that are equidistant from one another. These color groupings are especially youthful and invigorating since they appear to contain every color of the rainbow! Here are the two colorways.

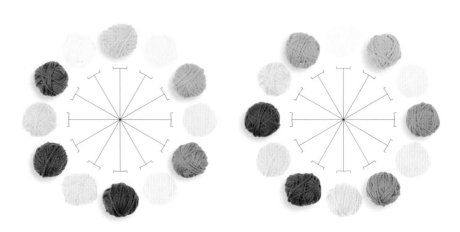

Designer's Workshop: Putting Color Theory into Practice

Of course, all this technical information about color theory looks great on paper and might even be fascinating, but as knitters, we're most interested in how the subject relates to yarn and our knitted projects. As a three-dimensional object, yarn presents colors differently than an artist's flat canvas. As you play with color, be sure to knit swatches to see your ideas come to life!

Here are some things to keep in mind as you choose and combine your colors:

• A successful color palette requires the right balance between colors. Extremely bright colors, for example, can overwhelm other colors within a design. Keep in mind, too, that any yarn with metallic qualities will dominate a colorway. Be sure to use strong colors and special yarns as accents to highlight particular areas in a design.

• Color contrast can make or break a pattern's readability, especially when knitting a pictorial motif. Always knit a swatch of your pattern to be sure there's enough contrast between the background and pattern colors to provide definition. Similarly, if you're adding a variegated or hand-painted yarn to a colorway, be sure to contrast it properly against other yarns; otherwise, the variegated yarn will disappear into the pattern.

• Subtle shadings in tonal colorways might be lost unless enough of each one is used. The key is balance and proportion.

• Heather and tweed yarns possess unique color qualities that are best used singly or with other yarns of the same category. If knitted along with solid colors, these beautiful yarns could become lost.

• Hairy or fuzzy yarns such as mohair or angora will blur the spots where color changes occur, creating a subtle effect.

• Bright and light colors tend to come forward visually in a design, so place these colors where you want to draw attention. Dark colors often seem to recede.

• Colors are affected by other colors within a project. If you place any color adjacent to a lighter color, it will appear darker. Position colors carefully to make sure that each one "pops" within your design.

• Be careful when working with whites, as they can make other colors look gray or dirty.

• When substituting colors, maintain the integrity of the original design by choosing colors of the same value: Swap your chosen light colors for the light colors in the original design and medium or dark colors for medium or dark colors.

• A good (and fun) way to choose a completely different colorway is simply to substitute each color in the original with its direct complement. You might be pleasantly surprised with the result!

• Take the time to launder your knitted swatch to be sure that the colors don't bleed. Commercial products that prevent excess dye from one section of a project from running into others—such as Retayne™ color fixative, Carbona Dye Grabber™, and Shout® Color Catcher® dryer sheets—are available.

Remember that although color is a scientific phenomenon based on physics, our preference for one color over another or this grouping over that one is subjective. With no absolute rules about right and wrong, colorwork provides the perfect venue for personalizing your knitting. Just think of color theory as another tool in your knitting backpack, and have fun!

2 Mastering Color Knitting Techniques Using Stripes

Knitters create multicolor patterns the exact same way they do simple, solid-colored fabrics—one stitch at a time. Learn just a few key techniques and you'll be able to produce beautiful colorwork, from stripes to graphic patterns to exciting, colorful textures, many of which appear much more complicated than they really are. With some basic tips and methods, from attaching new colors of yarn to managing several balls of yarn at once and minimizing tails, you'll avoid frustration and gain a firm foundation for all types of color knitting. To see these techniques in action, we'll knit one color per row and create simple yet stunning color patterns—with stripes!

Stripes are the obvious introduction to multicolor knitting: just change yarns at the start

of a row and the colorplay begins. Vary the colors according to a pattern—you can even

design your own (see page 53 for suggestions)—to create fabric that's fun and easy to knit.

If you're like me, simple stripes offer that "just one more row" kind of knitting; I always want

to add just one more stripe to see what the effect is going to be! In this section, we'll start

with basic stripes and then add textured interest with ripples, lace, tuck stitches, and more.

Stripes using slipped stitches are interesting—and exciting—enough to warrant their own

chapter (page 84).

Starting a New Color
To begin a new yarn color, drop the working yarn at the beginning of a knit row. Insert your right-hand needle into the first stitch of the row as if you are about to knit and, leaving a 6" [15cm] tail, grab the new yarn and use it to knit the first stitch (illustration 1).

The new color is now your working yarn. Of course, you can start a new color within any stitch pattern in the same way. To begin a new color on a purl row, for example, simply insert the right-hand needle into the first stitch of the row as if you're about to purl, and purl the first stitch.

NOTE: *Although beginning and ending with at least a 6"/[15cm] long yarn tail may seem cumbersome, it's essential for successful color knitting; if the tail is too short, it will be difficult to weave in, and the join may come apart as you knit. Fortunately, those tails will come in handy when it is time to sew seams. Use a tail rather than a new strand of yarn for seaming—that's one less pesky tail to weave in!*

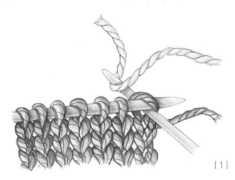

[1]

Carrying Yarn

As you knit a pattern, you may be changing colors quite frequently. It might seem then that you must cut each yarn as you work and start with a new strand every time you change colors. However, any knitter will tell you that it's best (or most effective, at least) to minimize the number of yarn tails in a knitted fabric whenever possible. Depending on the number of rows or stitches that a color will not be in use, you may be able to carry the yarn from one area of the fabric to the next without cutting it, thereby reducing the number of yarn tails. Of course, when knitting in the round, it is easiest to carry the yarn loosely along the "seam," or end of each round, on the wrong side of the fabric until needed.

To pick up and knit with a yarn that is already attached to your fabric, simply drop the old color and grasp the new one, bringing the new color *from underneath* the old one as you begin the row (illustration 2). Picking up the new yarn from underneath is the standard technique, but it sometimes contributes to tangling among the skeins or balls of yarn in use. If this happens to you, try alternating the direction of pick-up— grabbing one from underneath and the next from above—as you switch colors. As you knit with the new color, be sure to keep your tension as even as possible, and avoid the temptation to yank on the yarn tightly. Otherwise, the edge might pucker and distort the shape of the fabric.

When working patterns that are four or more rows high, it's a good idea to catch the unused color with the working yarn every few rows to prevent creating long yarn strands that might

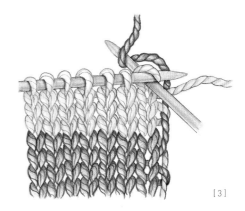

[3]

snag as you work (illustration 3). As before, grab the new yarn from underneath the old one, or alternate the pick-up, and maintain even tension as you work.

The Knit-Turn and Knit-Slide Principles

When changing colors at the end of a row, as when knitting stripes, you'll need to make sure that the yarn is at the proper side of the fabric so you can pick up and knit the color you need when the pattern requires it. In flat knitting (not in the round), the fabric is turned at the end of each row. But what happens if a yarn color used in Row 1 (waiting on the left of the knitting) needs to be picked up to begin Row 4 (on the right of the knitting)? To avoid such problems, it's good to know what I call the knit-turn and knit-slide principles.

[2]

Take a look at your pattern chart. Is each color used for an even number of rows, an odd number of rows, or both?

For an even number of rows *per color*, use the knit-turn principle. Simply knit with straight one-end needles, turning the work as you would for flat single-color knitting. Carry the yarns loosely up the side as you go.

For an odd number of rows *per color*, use the knit-slide principle with double-pointed needles or a circular needle, which allow you to knit off whichever end of the needle you choose. For single row stripes, for example, simply knit across one row with your first color, and then slide the stitches back to the beginning of the needle. Then, use your second color to knit across these stitches. Because you have not turned the work, both rows are right side rows. Continue to knit and slide stitches *without turning the fabric* according to the color pattern. When you are ready to begin the pattern repeat, turn the work and begin the pattern, working single purl rows for each color in succession. You are now working on wrong side rows. Carry the unused yarns loosely up the side as described above. You may find that the ends of rows become bulky, but those carried yarns will be hidden in the seams of your garment.

color PLAY

When designing your own stripe pattern, chart it out on a sheet of graph paper to determine when the yarns can be carried. With some clever planning, you can change the sequence to make your knitting—and your finishing—more efficient.

This sample chart demonstrates the knit-slide principle. Here, the pattern uses four colors in single-row stripes. The red arrows indicate the direction of knitting for each row.

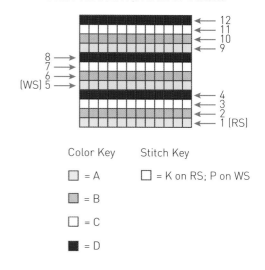

SINGLE ROW STRIPES USING AN EVEN NUMBER OF COLORS

Color Key

☐ = A

▨ = B

☐ = C

■ = D

Stitch Key

☐ = K on RS; P on WS

If a particular yarn is out of use for many stitches or rows, usually about 1" (2.5cm) or more, you might prefer to cut and reattach it later.

For a combination of odd and even number rows, use your judgment for which principle best applies. Sometimes the yarns can be carried up the sides of the fabric, and other times they'll have to be cut. Being flexible in this way will also allow you to adapt your knitting to whatever garment or pattern you choose. For example, when shaping armoles and neck openings, you'll have to suspend the knit-slide technique to bind off stitches at the beginning of rows. In these cases, bite the bullet and cut the yarn. Your beautiful, symmetrically shaped garment pieces will be worth it. You can resume the knit-slide technique after you have completed the bind-offs.

Color Knitting in the Round

When knitting circularly, color patterns can cause a noticeable jog in the fabric where the beginning and end of the round meet, as shown in the stockinette stitch example (below left).

Following are two tricks to help hide the jog. Try both to see which you prefer!

The first option is to use slipped stitches. It's easy and quick and may seem an intuitive solution to many knitters. On the first round of each new color, knit around, doing nothing to hide the jog. On the second round of each color, slip the first stitch of the new round purlwise without knitting it, and then knit the rest of the stripe as normal. The slipped stitch pulls up the beginning and the end of the round to the same height to disguise the shift in colors (below center).

Another option is to knit the first stitch of the second round *in the row below* (below right). This technique might feel slightly awkward at first, but it does a good job of hiding the jog. On the first round of each new color, knit around as usual, doing nothing out of the ordinary to hide

color PLAY

When knitting in the round, an odd- or even-number of rows/rounds per color doesn't matter. It's easy just to pull up the desired color to the height you need it. For wide patterns, you will want to twist the yarns together every few rounds so the vertical strands don't become unwieldy.

the jog. On the second round of each color, knit the first stitch of the round in the row below and then continue normally for the rest of the stripe. Working the first stitch of the round this way blends the beginning and end of the rounds together, hiding the jog.

Note that each of the tricks requires that your stripe is at least two rounds high. If your stripe is only one row, you can often wiggle the fabric as you deal with the yarn tails to even out the jog.

Left: Color knitting in the round produces a noticeable jog in the fabric. **Center:** Slipped stitches minimize the appearance of the jog. **Right:** Working stitches in the row below also helps to hide the jog.

Dealing with Yarn Tails

Needless to say, when knitting any type of colorwork, including stripes, numerous yarn tails will accumulate. There are ways to handle them. Many knitters like to save finishing time by knitting their ends in as they go, especially if they're working on a very complex color pattern. After all, who doesn't want to be finished with a project as soon as it comes off the needles! Others choose to weave in all their yarn tails at once when their project is completed. Choose the method that makes you happiest as a knitter.

Weaving In As You Knit

When working yarn tails into the fabric as you knit, it's a good idea to weave the old tail across the first stripe of the new color. Then work across the next row normally. When you turn to work the third row of the new stripe, you can easily weave in that first tail of the new stripe as you go. This method is slightly different for Continental- and American-style knitting, although for both styles the tail is held in the nonworking hand (your right hand if you're a Continental-style knitter or in your left hand if you're an American-style thrower). As always, it's a good idea to allow for 6"/[15cm] tails. Anything shorter than this will be difficult to weave in.

American style: Bring the yarn tail *under* the working yarn as you knit or purl the first stitch. For the second stitch, bring the old yarn tail *over* the working yarn as you knit or purl the stitch. Continue in this fashion, bringing the old yarn alternately under and over the working yarn on the wrong side of the fabric for approximately 2"/ [5cm]. Snip the tail, leaving ½"/[13mm].

Continental style: Work the first stitch per your pattern, then work the second stitch as follows. Insert the right-hand needle into this stitch as usual, then, before working the stitch, bring the yarn tail *over* the working yarn and around the right-hand needle tip counterclockwise; wrap the working yarn around the needle as usual, then

Minimizing Yarn Tails

To minimize as many yarn tails as possible when working with wool yarns, use spit splicing to join yarn ends of the same color. To do this: Unravel the plies on both tails for about 3–6"/[7.5–15cm]; break off half of the plies for each one and then fluff out the fibers of the remaining plies of each of the yarns. Dampen your hands, overlap the two ends, and rub your hands together with the two yarns between them for about 30 seconds. The friction will felt the hairy fibers of the yarns together. (If working with three-ply yarn, use one ply from one yarn and two plies from the other.)

If your yarn is not 100 percent wool, use the Russian join as follows: Make a loop in one of the yarn ends by threading its tail onto a pointed-end yarn needle and drawing it back through 1 to 2"/ [2.5–5cm] of itself, making certain it's woven within the plies of the yarn; remove the needle, leaving the loop. Thread the second yarn tail onto the needle and draw it through the loop of the first yarn tail to interlock them. Run this yarn back through its own plies, as you did the first tail, then tug on the ends and trim them.

unwrap the tail back to its original position; finally, pull the working yarn through the stitch and onto the right-hand needle. Continue alternating the first and second stitches in this fashion for approximately 2"/[5cm]. Snip the tail, leaving ½"/[13mm].

As you weave in the tails, take care to maintain the regular tension of the knitting. If it seems that these sections are slightly tighter than the rest of the fabric, gently tug widthwise to even out the fabric.

NOTE: *It's important to leave a ½"/[13mm] tail after weaving in ends. If you make them any shorter, the tail may poke out on the right side of the fabric. If necessary, you can always use a crochet hook to pull the end back to the inside of the garment.*

Weaving In to Finish

Here's an easy method to weave in any yarn tails that remain after a project has been knitted. Be sure to work each tail individually, in opposite diagonal directions, and you will secure your yarn ends while keeping the public side (the side that faces the outside) of your fabric beautiful.

On the wrong side of the fabric, thread the yarn tail through the eye of a pointed-end yarn needle. Then sew into the plies of adjoining stitches in a diagonal line for about 1"/[2.5cm] or so. To lock these short running stitches in place, work back through adjacent stitches toward the base of the yarn tail, leaving at least 2"/[5cm] of the tail loose. To secure, work a stitch or two as before and then pierce the plies of these final stitches with running stitches. Trim any excess tail to about ½"/[13mm].

NOTE: *To keep the weaving as invisible as possible, keep the tails on the wrong side of the fabric as you sew, being careful not to pierce the fabric itself.*

Incorporating Yarn Tails into Fringe

If your project calls for a fringed edge, it's easy to work your remaining yarn tails into the fringe. Just include the tails into each tuft as you loop the fringe. Pull tight and trim evenly. Sneaky? Sure. But it minimizes the number of yarn tails to weave in!

color PLAY

It's important to carry the yarns *loosely* up the side of the fabric. Tight floats cause the fabric to pucker and to lose its elasticity lengthwise. When knitting pieces to be sewn together as a garment, we don't need to worry about those floating strands looking messy, because they're usually hidden inside seams.

Sometimes, however, the sides of the fabric will show, as in a scarf or afghan project. To turn the floating strands into an asset, twist the yarns every few rows to create a decorative edge (illustration 4). If you do need to cut the floats, you can weave in the tails as you knit or after you've finished the garment. Or, better yet, you can incorporate those tails into fringe, turning what might have been a finishing nuisance into a design element!

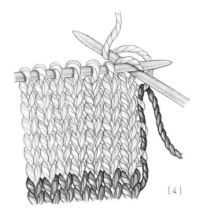

[4]

Common Stitch Patterns

Stitch patterns affect the appearance of color patterns, even those as simple as knitted stripes. And you can apply practically any stitch you like to striped designs. (Turn to the Pattern Treasury of Striped Stitches on page 53 for proof!) Still, sometimes the simplest of stitches shows off a pattern or design most effectively—especially when a complex color palette is used. From stockinette to garter stitch, to ribbing and more, common stitches and stripes create dynamic fabrics that are anything but boring.

Stockinette Stitch

This common fabric is created by alternating one knit row with one purl row (or by knitting every round when working circularly). Each side of the fabric looks completely different; the knit side appears smooth, and the purl side looks bumpy. Stripes look quite different in stockinette and reverse stockinette stitch fabrics, although one is, of course, simply the back side of the other. In the photograph below left, color changes appear crisp in stockinette stitch, but in the reverse stockinette stitch shown in the photograph below right, the stripes blend into each other in a subtler way.

Garter Stitch

Most beginning knitters love garter stitch because all rows are worked the same way— by knitting every stitch—resulting in a highly textured, reversible fabric. Once stripes are introduced, however, the fabric appears different on each side. Typically, striped garter stitch designs change colors on even-numbered rows. This technique creates neat horizontal ridges for each stripe on one side of the fabric, below left. On the reverse side of the same swatch, the stripes are blurred, below right.

Above: Color changes appear crisp in stockinette stitch (left) and blended in reverse stockinette stitch (right), even though one swatch is simply the back side of the other.

Above: Color changes in garter stitch change the look of the fabric on each side. On one side the stripes appear crisp (left), and on the reverse side the colors appear blended.

color PLAY

Any combination of stockinette and garter stitch can be used to create striped designs. If you want sharp, clearly defined stripes, be sure that the first row of each color is *knitted* on a right-side row or *purled* on a wrong-side row. Doing the opposite will create blurred stripes.

Combining Stitches for Texture

Stripes allow for plenty of creativity, even when using common stitches such as stockinette and garter. Each stitch brings its own unique properties to a design, and you can mix and match stitches as you like to create one-of-a-kind striped patterns.

Stockinette Stitch with Garter Ridges

Here, I've combined stockinette stitch with contrasting colored garter stitch stripes to create a nice textured effect. In this fabric, three-row garter stitch stripes (Rows 7–10 and 17–20) create textured horizontal ridges.

You can make garter stitch ridges appear more or less prominent in a design simply by changing the number of garter stitch rows. For example, fewer rows of garter stitch create finer horizontal ridges (below). It's easy to see in the chart for this fabric that Rows 5–6 and 11–12 create the contrasting narrow horizontal ridges.

STOCKINETTE STITCH WITH WIDE GARTER RIDGES

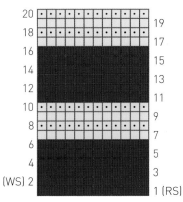

Color Key

■ = A

□ = B

Stitch Key

□ = K on RS; p on WS

• = K on WS

STOCKINETTE STITCH WITH NARROW GARTER RIDGES

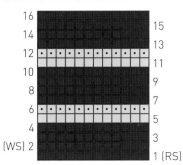

Color Key

■ = A

□ = B

Stitch Key

□ = K on RS; p on WS

• = K on WS

Stockinette Stitch with Reverse Stockinette Welts

This combination of stitch patterns produces a profoundly textured fabric; the reverse stockinette stitch stripes "pop" on the flat stockinette stitch ground (below). As with ribbings, it's a good idea to knit the first row of the reverse stockinette stitch stripes on the right side (or purl them on the wrong side) to avoid little blips of the wrong color from showing up where you don't want them on the fabric. In the chart for this swatch, Rows 7–10 and 17–20 create highly embossed horizontal welts.

STOCKINETTE STITCH WITH REVERSE STOCKINETTE STITCH WELTS

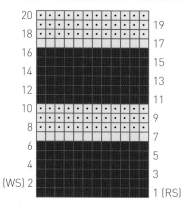

Color Key

■ = A

□ = B

Stitch Key

□ = K on RS; p on WS

• = K on WS

Ribbings

Ribbed fabrics are comprised of vertical alignments of knit and purl stitches. Add stripes to the mix and things get interesting. As we've seen earlier in stripes worked in reverse stockinette stitch (page 38), color changes on purl stitches create blurred lines, which can present a problem when working ribbing. (Of course, sometimes you'll want blips of the alternate color to show, but we'll get into that with slip stitches in Chapter 3.)

For perfectly smooth color changes, ignore your rib pattern on the first row of each new color. In other words, for each stripe's first row, knit all stitches on right-side rows and purl all stitches on wrong-side rows. Don't worry about the fabric losing its elasticity; one little row of knit stitches won't affect it much, but be sure to reestablish the rib pattern on the second row of each stripe.

Above: Whether colors change on purl stitches (left) or on knit stitches (right) dramatically affects the crispness of the stripe pattern.

Fancy Stitch Patterns

Although I love the bright, graphic sensibility that even the simplest stitches lend to stripes, as a designer I'm sometimes looking for a new take on stripes. In fact, many beautiful stitch patterns are worked in stripes but employ certain techniques to disrupt the "stripy-ness" in interesting, unexpected ways. Ripple stitches, stitches worked into rows below, and tuck stitch patterns all comprise a fun, basic set of fancy stitch patterns to get you started; other striped stitch pattern variations can be found in the Pattern Treasury of Striped Stitches (page 53).

Ripple Patterns

Stripes show off the undulating waves of ripple patterns such as Feather and Fan (also known as Old Shale Pattern) using only a vertical alignment of increases and decreases to marvelous effect. Wherever there's a concentration of increases, the fabric points upward; a grouping of decreases pushes the fabric downward.

The following swatch and chart illustrate this principle in an 11-stitch repeat. Fabric knit from just one repeat of this chart will be shaped like a V, with the center of the piece pointed downward

color PLAY

Ripple patterns are some of the easiest, and the most fun, striped patterns to design. Try adding rows of garter stitch or bobbles for texture. Or vary the place in the pattern where you change colors for stripes. Just be sure to maintain your stitch count; for every increase there should be a corresponding decrease. See the Pattern Treasury of Striped Stitches (page 53) for additional examples.

where decreases are stacked on top of one another on every other row. If you cast on any multiple of 11 stitches—say 33 stitches, 121 stitches, or even 2,277 stitches—and work this chart, your fabric will "magically" ripple.

RIPPLE PATTERN

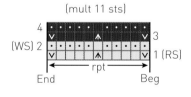

(mult 11 sts)

(WS) 2

1 (RS)

rpt

End   Beg

Color Key

□ = A

■ = B

Stitch Key

□ = K on RS; p on WS

· = K on WS

∨ = (Increase from 1 st to 2 sts) = K into front and then into back of st

⋀ = S2kp2 = Central Double Decrease = Slip 2 sts at once knitwise; k1; p2sso

color PLAY

The swatches shown in this chapter present horizontal stripes. If you prefer vertical stripes in your project, simply invert your knitting. Easy! That's why the Nubby Stripes Cardi (page 74) is knitted sideways.

Dip Stitch Patterns

This type of striped pattern adds a vertical element to the mix, creating an elongated stitch that connects an earlier row to the current one. With this stitch pattern, stripes appear dramatically less horizontal—a definite plus when knitting and designing garments in petite or plus sizes.

To create a dip stitch pattern, insert the right-hand needle several rows below the next stitch on the left-hand needle (illustration 5) and draw up an elongated loop, leaving it on the right-hand needle (illustration 6). Knit the next stitch the

usual way (illustration 7). Then, to maintain the correct stitch count, pass the elongated stitch over the stitch just knitted as if you're binding it off (illustration 8).

NOTE: *When working dip stitch patterns, don't worry about how loose those elongated stitches seem at first. They even out after you pass them over the subsequent stitches.*

In the chart for the sample fabric, the dip stitches in Rows 3 and 7 are worked six rows down to create the elongated stitches. Each pattern will indicate how far below you should work.

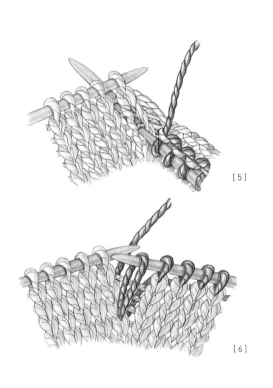

[5]

[6]

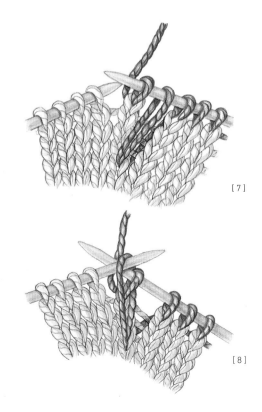

[7]

[8]

DIP STITCH PATTERN

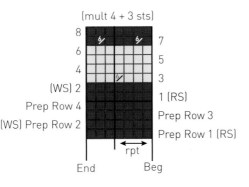

(mult 4 + 3 sts)

Color Key

■ = A

□ = B

Stitch Key

□ = K on RS; p on WS

У = Elongated Dip St = Insert RH needle into st 6 rows below, and draw up a st, leaving it on RH needle; k next st; pass the Elongated Dip St over the knitted st

Patterns Using Stitches Worked in the Rows Below

Working stitches into the row or rows below creates a beautiful, soft, crochetlike fabric. For this technique, rather than work into the stitch that's sitting on the left-hand needle, insert the right-hand needle into the stitch *one row below* and then knit the stitch the regular way. As you pull the working yarn through to create a new stitch, you catch both the "row below" stitch and the stitch that you would normally knit on the right-hand needle.

NOTE: *Stitches worked into rows below tend to draw in heightwise because of the vertical movement of the stitches. As a result, these types of fabrics may seem to spread out widthwise naturally. Before planning a project using this type of stitch pattern, carefully measure your gauge on a swatch worked in your desired stitch pattern.*

In the chart for the pattern shown below, the stitches that are worked in the row below reach down into stitches in the second color, resulting in a fabric that almost looks crocheted.

STITCH WORKED IN THE ROW BELOW PATTERN

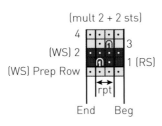

(mult 2 + 2 sts)

Color Key

■ = A

□ = B

Stitch Key

□ = K on RS; p on WS

• = P on RS; k on WS

∩ = Knit st in the row below

Tuck Stitch Patterns

In this type of pattern, a stitch is unraveled for a number of rows, then the stitch and all the horizontal ladders created from the unraveling are knitted together. This technique creates decidedly un-stripy fabrics with interesting texture.

Machine knitters know how wonderful tuck stitch patterns are, and it's easy to duplicate the look in hand knitting. Don't let the idea of dropping stitches to unravel them scare you: I promise they won't go far!

To create a tuck stitch pattern, drop the first stitch off the left-hand needle (illustration 9) and use the tip of the right-hand needle to unravel the specified number of rows (illustration 10). Then insert the right-hand needle into the live stitch, catching the horizontal strands on top of the needle (illustration 11). Finally, knit into the live stitch, working all those strands into the new stitch (illustration 12).

[9]

[11]

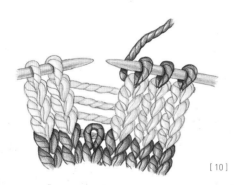

[10]

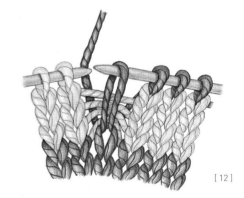

[12]

In the chart for this swatch, tuck stitches are worked on blue rows only, with the intermittent yellow rows unraveled and then gathered up.

color **PLAY**

Many charts include prep, or preparation, rows, which function exactly as the name suggests. This type of row prepares your knitting for the pattern stitches. The preparation row is worked only once and is not included in the pattern repeat.

TUCK STITCH PATTERN

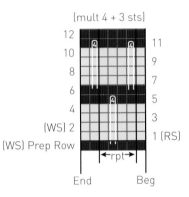

(mult 4 + 3 sts)

Color Key

■ = A

□ = B

Stitch Key

□ = K on RS; p on WS

= Tuck St = Drop st off LH needle and, using tip of RH needle, unravel 4 rows down; insert RH needle into the live st and knit it, catching the 4 loose strands into the st as you knit

Left: Stripe Pattern 18 (page 61) shows off a two-color design in which both knit and purl stitches are unraveled and tucked. **Right:** The three-color Stripe Pattern 16 (page 60), tucks only knit stitches, resulting in a flatter, less textured fabric.

Mitered Motifs

Mitered motifs aren't exactly a type of stitch pattern; but they do show off stripes in an interesting way, even when worked in simple garter stitch, as shown in most of my examples. Of course, garter stitch also means no curling at the edges. But for me, the best part of mitered patterns is that each motif is built on those that are already knit, so there's minimal finishing at the end. And as a bonus, mitered motifs are a great way to use up scrap yarn.

There are three simple things to remember when knitting mitered motifs:

1) Slip the first stitch knitwise in every row.

2) Purl the last stitch in every row.

3) Use the knit-on cast-on technique throughout: Begin with a slip knot on your needle. Insert the tip of the right-hand needle knitwise into the loop that's sitting on the left-hand needle (illustration 13) and knit a stitch *without removing the original stitch from the left-hand needle* (illustration 14); instead, transfer the new stitch from the right-hand needle back to the left-hand one. One new stitch has been cast on. Repeat for each successive stitch to be cast on.

All mitered motifs use this knit-on cast-on technique to build motifs upon one another and can be worked in any number of stitch patterns to create texture as well as a diagonal design. Use an even number of stitches to create a subtle diagonal design or an odd number of stitches to create a prominent diagonal design and to add texture.

NOTE: *To change the size of a basic motif, use the knit-on cast-on technique to cast on any even number of stitches, and place a marker between the two middle stitches on Row 1. To change the size of any motif with a prominent or textured diagonal design (such as either of the following two motifs), cast on any odd number of stitches and place a marker on the center stitch on Row 1. Complete both types of motifs following the mitered motif technique.*

[13]

[14]

Subtle Diagonals with Even Stitches

(This example is worked in garter stitch on 28 stitches and uses two colors: A and B)

Row 1 (RS): With A, using the knit-on cast-on technique throughout, cast on (or pick up and knit if you are attaching motifs) 14 stitches, then place a marker to indicate the center. Cast on (or pick up and knit if you are attaching motifs) 14 more stitches—28 stitches total.

Row 2: Slip the first stitch knitwise, knit across to the last stitch, p1.

Row 3: With B, slip the first stitch knitwise, knit across to 2 stitches before the marker, k2tog, slip the marker, ssk, knit across to the last stitch, p1—26 stitches.

Row 4: As for Row 2.

Rows 5 and 6: With A, work the same as Rows 3 and 4—24 stitches.

Repeat Rows 3–6 until 4 stitches remain, ending after a wrong-side row.

Next Row: K2tog, ssk.

Next Row: As for Row 2.

Next Row: Remove the marker, k2tog.

Fasten off.

Prominent Diagonals with Odd Stitches

(This example is worked in garter stitch on 29 stitches and uses two colors: A and B)

Row 1 (RS): With A, using the knit-on cast-on technique throughout, cast on (or pick up and knit if you are attaching motifs) 15 stitches, then place a marker on the last stitch to indicate that it will be the corner stitch. Cast on (or pick up and knit) 14 more stitches—29 stitches total.

Row 2: Slip the first stitch knitwise, knit across to the marked center stitch, p1, knit across to the last stitch, ending the row with p1.

Row 3: With B, slip the first stitch knitwise, knit across to 1 stitch before the marked center stitch, s2kp2, knit across to the last stitch, ending the row with p1—27 stitches.

Row 4: As for Row 2.

Rows 5 and 6: With A, work the same as Rows 3 and 4—25 stitches.

Repeat Rows 3–6 until 3 stitches remain.

Next Row (WS): As for Row 2.

Next Row: S2kp2.

Fasten off.

Above: An even number of stitches creates a subtle diagonal design for mitered motifs.

Above: An odd number of stitches creates a prominent diagonal design for mitered motifs.

Textured Diagonal Designs

(This example is worked in stockinette stitch with scattered garter stitch ridges on 29 stitches and uses two colors: A and B)

Row 1 (RS): With A, using the knit-on cast-on technique throughout, cast on (or pick up and knit if you are attaching motifs) 15 stitches, then place a marker on the last stitch to indicate that it will be the corner stitch. Cast on (or pick up and knit) 14 more stitches—29 stitches total.

Row 2: Slip the first stitch knitwise, knit across to the marked center stitch, p1, knit across to the last stitch, ending the row with p1.

Row 3: With B, slip the first stitch knitwise, knit across to 1 stitch before the marked center stitch, s2kp2, knit across to the last stitch, ending the row with p1.

Row 4: Slip the first stitch knitwise, purl across to the end of the row.

Row 5: With A, work the same as for Row 3.

Row 6: Slip the first stitch knitwise, knit across to the end of the row.

Repeat Rows 3–6 until 3 stitches remain.

Next Row (WS): As for Row 2.

Next Row: S2kp2.

Fasten off.

Above: Combining common stitch patterns creates a fabric with even more texture, as shown by this stockinette stitch and garter stitch–based fabric with a prominent diagonal design.

Joining Motifs

Subsequent motifs build upon one another, using the knit-on cast-on technique, depending on their location within the overall design. In the example shown here, a subtle diagonal design runs from the lower left to the upper right of the motif. When building one motif onto another, the first set of stitches is picked up directly into one edge of the previous motif. To pick up and knit, insert the right-hand needle into a stitch (or into the side of a row) and knit a new stitch (illustration 15). If the subsequent motif forms an edge of the design, simply cast on stitches for the other half of the first row (illustration 16). If you're knitting a motif with a prominent diagonal, be sure to add one center stitch for the corner.

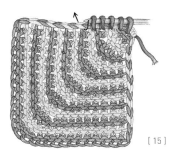

[15]

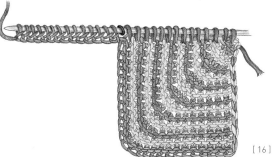

[16]

CONSTRUCTION DIAGRAM

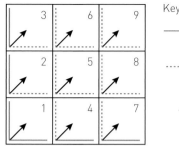

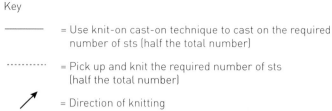

Key

——————— = Use knit-on cast-on technique to cast on the required number of sts (half the total number)

·············· = Pick up and knit the required number of sts (half the total number)

↗ = Direction of knitting

Motifs can be constructed vertically or horizontally, with subsequent strips added until the design is complete. In the construction diagram, Motif 2 is worked vertically onto Motif 1, and Motif 3 is then worked onto Motif 2 before proceeding to Motif 4.

To join a motif above an existing motif (such as Motif 2 in Construction Diagram, above):
With the right side of the existing motif facing you, pick up and knit the first half of the stitches along the upper edge of the existing motif, then use the knit-on cast-on technique to cast on the second half of the stitches. Begin with Row 2 and complete the same as for the first motif.

To join a motif to the right side of an existing motif (such as Motif 4 in Construction Diagram, above):
After an entire vertical strip of motifs has been knitted, the next strip is knitted onto it. For the first motif of this second strip (Motif 4 in the Construction Diagram), begin by using the knit-on cast-on technique to cast on the first half of the stitches, place a marker, then with the right side of the existing motif facing you, pick up and knit the second half of the stitches along the right-hand edge of the first motif of the other strip. Begin with Row 2 and complete the same as for the first motif.

To join a motif to two existing motifs (such as Motif 5 in Construction Diagram, above):
With the right side of the existing motif facing you, pick up and knit the first half of the stitches along the upper edge of the existing motif, then with the right side of the existing motif facing you, pick up and knit the second half of the stitches along the right-hand edge of the other motif. Begin with Row 2 and complete the same as for the first motif.

color PLAY

Of course, it's possible to knit mitered motifs with the diagonal design going from lower right to upper left. The construction of this motif would be a mirror image of the Construction Diagram example discussed at length in this section. Motifs at a garment's edge will be added by first casting on half of the necessary stitches and then picking up and knitting the other half of the stitches onto previous motifs. As with the previous example, motifs should be constructed vertically, with subsequent vertical strips added until the design is complete.

Designer's Workshop:
Designing with Lines

The actual knitting of stripes may be pretty simple, but a well-planned design—in color, sequence, and construction—doesn't just happen. Fortunately, stripes are infinitely adaptable, and their patterns are a great deal of fun to develop. As you embark on new combinations of stripes, keep in mind the elements of color theory from Chapter 1, as well as the following ideas that may help you get started on designs of your own—and help you incorporate them into your knitting projects.

Inventing (and Playing with) Striping Sequences

Simple horizontal stripes may seem like the most basic of motifs, but the possibilities for designs are limitless. When designing, you may choose to stick to some of the examples presented in this chapter, or you may wish to mix things up by combining narrow stripes with wider ones. You may even want to create designs inspired by the projects in this book. Joan's Hoodie (page 68), for example, showcases a fun, whimsical look created by a long pattern involving stripes of varying heights.

How to choose from the myriad options available? Rather than always taking the time to knit experimental swatches of stripe patterns, feel free to utilize the following shortcuts to experiment with color and stripes. Of course, once you've decided which one to use in your project, be sure to knit a swatch to make sure you like the colors and textures worked up.

• Cut a piece of cardboard to 4" x 11"/[10cm x 28cm]. Sample different stripe patterns by winding yarn in stripes of various widths around the cardboard. If you don't like the combination of color and stripe width, simply unwind it and start again!

• If you're computer savvy, use a spreadsheet or graphics program to play with colors and widths of stripes.

Stumped choosing a stripe pattern? Look to mathematics and technology for inspiration. (Who would ever have thought we'd be using so much science and math in our creative endeavors?)

• Try using the Fibonacci Sequence of numbers. Each number in the series is the sum of its two predecessors: 0, 1, 1, 2, 3, 5, 8, 13, 21, and so on. For example:

Stripe 1: 1 row
Stripe 2: 1 row
Stripe 3: 2 rows
Stripe 4: 3 rows
Stripe 5: 5 rows
Stripe 6: 8 rows
Stripe 7: 13 rows

At this point, you can repeat from Stripe 1 or else work backward from Stripe 6 to Stripe 1 and then repeat from the beginning. Of course, you can begin anywhere within the Fibonacci Sequence and use as many repeats as you like. Just keep in mind that it's difficult to support a gazillion colors per design!

• The Golden Mean is an irrational number that's been used for centuries by architects and artists to create aesthetically pleasing works. Believe it or not, even today's lowly 3" x 5"/[7.5cm x 12.5cm] index card fits into its proportional guidelines. The magic number is 1.618034. To develop a new stripe sequence, divide each stripe by the Golden Mean to come up with the next stripe height, like this:

Stripe 1: 10 rows
Stripe 2: 6 rows (= 10 ÷ 1.618034)
Stripe 3: 4 rows (= 6 ÷ 1.618034)
Stripe 4: 2 rows (= 4 ÷ 1.618034)
Stripe 5: 1 row (= 2 ÷ 1.618034)

Again, as in the last example, you can either begin again with Stripe 1 or reverse the sequence to complete one pattern.

• A fun way to develop new stripe patterns (and also a great way to waste time) is to play with an online stripe generator. There are many sites available, including www.kissyourshadow.com/stripe_maker.php and www.stripegenerator.com. Simply select, reject, change, and manipulate stripe colors, sizes, and patterns as you like until you find a design that works for your project.

Special Considerations

After you've chosen your stripe pattern, you'll still want to consider how best to implement it in a project. We've all heard the admonition to avoid horizontal stripes in clothing. It's an adage often proved true by unflattering garments that seem to emphasize the very areas we'd most like to hide. However, stripes do not have to mean fashion suicide, nor must they be relegated only to home decor. Instead, use the principles of color theory and stripe design to enhance a garment's—and a wearer's—beauty. Here are some tips:

• We know that warm colors tend to advance visually in a design, and cool colors seem to recede. In addition, the darker the color, the more likely it is to recede in a design. Experienced designers often place darker stripes and cooler colors toward the bottom of garments, with lighter, brighter, warmer colors toward the face of the wearer. Cleo's Jacket (page 136) is a great example of using light colors to attract the eye in this way. In general, try to place narrow, dark-colored stripes across parts of the body that you don't want emphasized. This clever use of colorblocking draws the eye away from any figure flaws. This trick is also helpful when designing for petite body frames.

• Nearly everyone knows that horizontal stripes tend to accentuate one's girth. One possible design option is to work the body of the garment side to side, shifting the direction of the stripes from horizontal to vertical.

• Sweaters are particularly pleasing to the eye when stripes match up along all pieces of the garment. When the sleeves and body have different lengths, some simple calculations are necessary to ensure that the stripes line up. The key is to have everything match at the point where the sleeves and body meet (illustration 17). An easy way to ensure that stripes line up is to knit the longer piece (usually the sleeve) first. Then, measure down from the armhole point of the sleeve to the desired length of the body. Note which color of the stripe pattern begins the sleeve and begin your front and back pieces with that stripe.

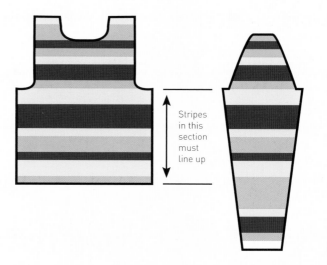

Stripes in this section must line up

Pattern Treasury of Striped Stitches

The following stripe patterns utilize different colors and textures to create fun striping effects like those discussed in this chapter. Each pattern includes a sample swatch and chart so that you can quickly find the perfect patterns for your projects. If you need a quick refresher course on chart reading or suggestions on how best to use this pattern treasury, turn to pages 144 and 149. I hope that this treasury inspires you to develop your own original patterns!

STRIPE PATTERN 1

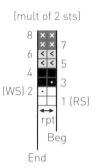

(mult of 2 sts)

Color Key

■ = A

□ = B

✕ = C

< = D

Stitch Key

□ = K on RS; p on WS

• = P on RS; k on WS

STRIPE PATTERN 2

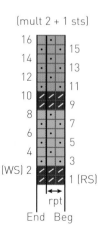

(mult 2 + 1 sts)

Color Key

◨ = A

▨ = B

▨ = C

Stitch Key

□ = K on RS; p on WS

• = P on RS; k on WS

STRIPE PATTERN 3

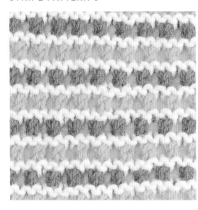

(mult 2 + 3 sts)

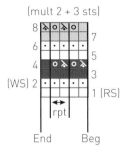

Color Key

□ = A

■ = B

▨ = C

Stitch Key

□ = K on RS; p on WS

• = K on WS

o = Yarn over

⋋ = K2tog on WS

STRIPE PATTERN 4

(mult 8 + 4 sts)

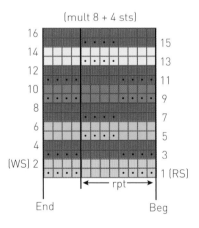

Color Key

▨ = A

■ = B

▨ = C

■ = D

□ = E

Stitch Key

□ = K on RS; p on WS

• = P on RS

STRIPE PATTERN 5

(4 + 2 sts)

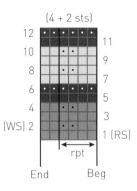

```
12  • • • • •    11
10    •   •       9
 8    •   •       7
 6  • • • • •     5
 4    •   •       3
(WS) 2  •   •    1 (RS)
```

← rpt →

End   Beg

Color Key

■ = A

■ = B

□ = C

Stitch Key

□ = K on RS; p on WS

• = P on RS; k on WS

STRIPE PATTERN 6

(mult 6 + 5 sts)

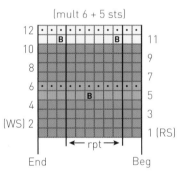

```
12  • • • • • • • •    
10     B         B      11
 8                     9
 6  • • • • • • • •    7
 4        B            5
(WS) 2                 3
                      1 (RS)
```

← rpt →

End   Beg

Color Key

■ = A

■ = B

□ = C

Stitch Key

□ = K on RS; p on WS

• = K on WS

B = Bobble = K into (front, back, front) of next st, turn; p1, (p1, yarn over, p1) all into next st, p1, turn; k5, turn; p2tog, p1, p2tog, turn; slip 2 sts at once knitwise, k1, p2sso

STRIPE PATTERN 7

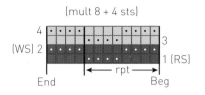

(mult 8 + 4 sts)

Color Key

■ = A

▨ = B

Stitch Key

□ = K on RS; p on WS

• = P on RS; k on WS

STRIPE PATTERN 8

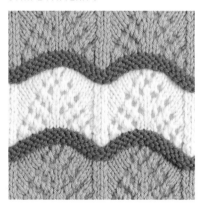

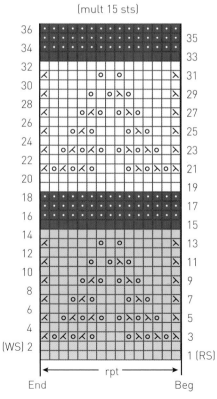

(mult 15 sts)

Color Key

▨ = A

■ = B

□ = C

Stitch Key

□ = K on RS; p on WS

• = P on RS; k on WS

○ = Yarn over

⟋ = K2tog on RS

⟍ = Ssk on RS

STRIPE PATTERN 9

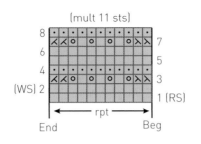

(mult 11 sts)

End   Beg

rpt

(WS) 2

Color Key

◻ = A

◻ = B

Stitch Key

◻ = K on RS; p on WS

• = K on WS

○ = Yarn over

⟋ = K2tog on RS

⟍ = Ssk on RS

STRIPE PATTERN 10

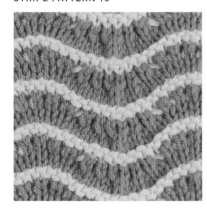

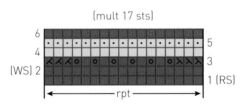

(mult 17 sts)

(WS) 2

1 (RS)

rpt

Color Key

■ = A

◻ = B

Stitch Key

◻ = K on RS; p on WS

• = P on RS; k on WS

○ = Yarn over

⟋ = K2tog on RS

⟍ = Ssk on RS

STRIPE PATTERN 11

(mult 11 sts)

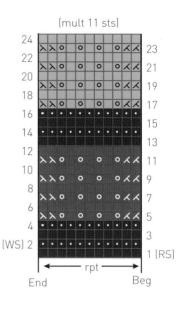

Color Key

■ = A

■ = B

■ = C

Stitch Key

□ = K on RS; p on WS

• = K on WS

○ = Yarn over

╱ = K2tog on RS

╲ = Ssk on RS

STRIPE PATTERN 12

(mult 6 + 5 sts)

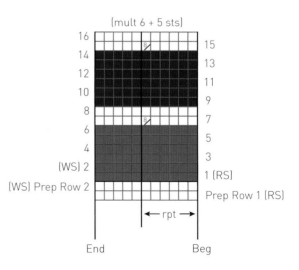

Color Key

□ = A

■ = B

■ = C

Stitch Key

□ = K on RS; p on WS

⅞╱ = Elongated Dip St = Insert RH needle into st 8 rows below and knit a st, leaving it on RH needle; k next st; pass the Elongated Dip St over the knitted st

STRIPE PATTERN 13

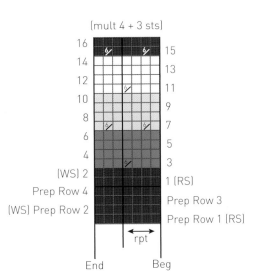

(mult 4 + 3 sts)

16 / 15
14 / 13
12 / 11
10 / 9
8 / 7
6 / 5
4 / 3
(WS) 2 / 1 (RS)
Prep Row 4 / Prep Row 3
(WS) Prep Row 2 / Prep Row 1 (RS)

rpt

End   Beg

Color Key

■ = A

■ = B

□ = C

□ = D

Stitch Key

□ = K on RS; p on WS

∠ = Elongated Dip St = Insert RH needle into st 6 rows below and knit a st, leaving
it on RH needle; k next st; pass the Elongated Dip St over the knitted st

---

STRIPE PATTERN 14

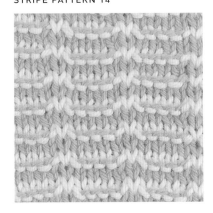

(mult 5 + 4 sts)

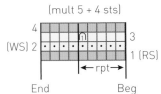

4 / 3
(WS) 2 / 1 (RS)

←rpt→

End   Beg

Color Key

■ = A

□ = B

Stitch Key

□ = K on RS; p on WS

• = P on RS; k on WS

∩ = Knit st in the row below

STRIPE PATTERN 15

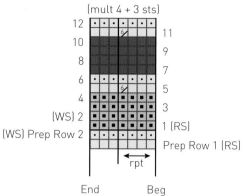

Color Key

■ = A

□ = B

■ = C

Stitch Key

□ = K on RS; p on WS

↘ = Elongated Dip St = Insert RH needle into st 6 rows below and knit a st, leaving it on RH needle; k next st; pass the Elongated Dip St over the knitted st

• = P on RS, k on WS

STRIPE PATTERN 16

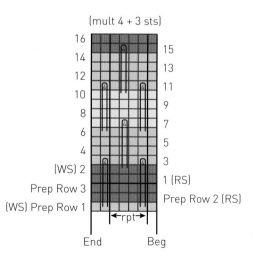

Color Key

■ = A

■ = B

■ = C

□ = D

Stitch Key

□ = K on RS; p on WS

⋒ = Tuck St = Drop st off LH needle and, using tip of RH needle, unravel 4 rows down; insert RH needle into the live st and knit it, catching the 4 loose strands into the st as you knit

STRIPE PATTERN 17

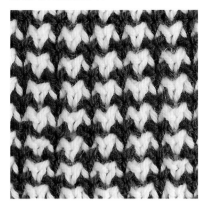

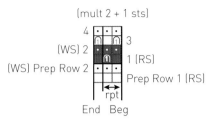

(mult 2 + 1 sts)

4
(WS) 2   3
(WS) Prep Row 2   1 (RS)
                Prep Row 1 (RS)
          rpt
End   Beg

Color Key

■ = A

□ = B

Stitch Key

□ = K on RS; p on WS

• = K on WS

∩ = Knit st in the row below

STRIPE PATTERN 18

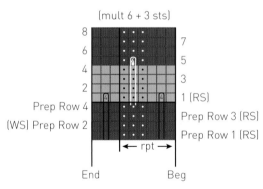

(mult 6 + 3 sts)

8   7
6   5
4   3
2   1 (RS)
Prep Row 4
(WS) Prep Row 2   Prep Row 3 (RS)
                     Prep Row 1 (RS)
          ← rpt →

End   Beg

Above: Right Side **Below:** Wrong Side

Color Key

■ = A

□ = B

Stitch Key

□ = K on RS; p on WS

• = P on RS; k on WS

= Tuck St = Drop st off LH needle and, using tip of RH needle, unravel 4 rows down; insert RH needle into the live st and knit it, catching the 4 loose strands into the st as you knit

= Textured Tuck St = Drop st off LH needle and, using tip of RH needle, unravel 4 rows down; insert RH needle into the live st and purl it, catching the 4 loose strands into the st as you purl

Striped Fingerless Mitts

Learning Color Knitting in the Round

These funky wristers are knitted entirely in the round using four colors of worsted weight yarn. Don these little lovelies and you can comfortably rake leaves—or even knit—outdoors on a cool autumn morning!

NOTES

- When changing colors, knit the first round of each color; on the subsequent round, reestablish the Rib Pattern.

- For quick and easy finishing, carry the yarns loosely up the inside after each stripe.

SUGGESTED ALTERNATE COLORWAYS

Alternate Colorway 1, left: Louet North America's *Gems Worsted* in Fern Green #39 (A), Goldilocks #05 (B), Caribbean Blue #14 (C), and Aqua #48 (D)

Alternate Colorway 2, right: Pure White #70 (A), Pink Panther #51 (B), Citrus Orange #62 (C), and Goldilocks #05 (D); (4)

SKILL LEVEL
Easy

SIZE
One size

FINISHED MEASUREMENTS
Circumference: 6½"/[16.5cm]

Length: 10"/[25.5cm]

MATERIALS
Louet North America's *Gems Worsted:* 4-medium/worsted weight; 100% superwash merino wool; each approximately 3½ oz/[100g] and 175 yd/ [160m]. 1 hank *each* of Citrus Orange #62 (A), Violet #45 (B), Caribbean Blue #14 (C), and Navy #56 (D); (4)

Size 7 (4.5mm) double-pointed needles (set of 4), or size needed to obtain gauge

Stitch marker

Stitch holder

Blunt-end yarn needle

GAUGE
32 stitches and 28 rounds = 4"/[10cm] in Rib Pattern.

To save time, take time to check gauge.

STITCH PATTERNS
Rib Pattern (multiple of 4 stitches)
Pattern Round (RS): *K2, p2; repeat from * around.

Stripe Pattern
Work the 18-round Stripe Pattern in Rib Pattern as follows: *2 rounds A, 3 rounds B, 4 rounds C, 2 rounds A, 3 rounds B, 4 rounds D; repeat from *.

Mitts (Make 2)

With A, cast on 52 stitches; divide evenly over 3 needles, place a marker for the beginning of the round, and join, being careful not to twist the stitches.

Begin the Rib Pattern and work even in the Stripe Pattern until the piece measures approximately 8"/[20.5cm].

DIVIDE FOR THUMB

Next Round: Work the first 5 stitches of the round in pattern as established and slip these stitches onto a holder, then work to the end of the round.

Next Round: Maintaining patterns as established, cast on 5 stitches, then work to the end of the round.

Continue even in patterns as established until the piece measures approximately 10"/[25.5cm] from the beginning.

Bind off *loosely* in pattern.

Thumb

With C, slip the 5 stitches from the holder onto a double-pointed needle, then pick up and knit 2 stitches along the first side edge of the thumb opening, pick up and knit the 5 stitches from the cast-on stitches over the thumb opening, then pick up and knit 1 stitch along the other side edge of the thumb opening—13 stitches total.

Divide these 13 stitches onto 3 double-pointed needles, place a marker for the beginning of the round, and reestablish the Rib Pattern as follows: k2, p2, k2, p3, k2, p2.

Continue even in pattern as established until the thumb measures approximately 1" [2.5cm].

Bind off *loosely* in pattern.

Weave in all yarn tails.

SKILL LEVEL
Easy

SIZES
Child's 2 (4, 6, 8). Instructions are for the smallest size, with changes for the other sizes noted in parentheses as necessary.

FINISHED MEASUREMENTS
Chest: 25½ (28, 31, 33½)"/ [65 (71, 79, 85)cm]

Length: 14½ (15½, 16½, 17½)"/ [37 (39.5, 42, 44.5)cm]

MATERIALS
Cascade Yarns' *Greenland*: 4-medium/ worsted weight; 100% superwash merino wool; each approximately 3½ oz/[100g] and 137 yd/[125m]. 2 (2, 3, 4) balls *each* of Lime #3525 (A), Teal #3518 (B), and Delft Blue #3508 (C); (4)

Size 6 (4mm) knitting needles

Size 6 (4mm) 16"/[40.5cm] circular needle

Size 8 (5mm) knitting needles, or size needed to obtain gauge

Two stitch markers

Blunt-end yarn needle

GAUGE
18 stitches and 28 rows = 4"/[10cm] in the Textured Stripe Pattern with larger needles.

To save time, take time to check gauge.

STITCH PATTERNS
Rib Pattern (odd number of stitches)
Row 1 (RS): K1, *p1, k1; repeat from * across.

Row 2: P1, *k1, p1; repeat from * across.

Repeat Rows 1 and 2 for the pattern.

Textured Stripe Pattern (multiple of 6 stitches + 5)
See chart (page 67).

Spring into Stripes Pullover

Combining Common Stitch Patterns with Stripes

Knit this great little sweater for every child on your gift list. It's easy to knit and fun to wear!

NOTES
- For ease in finishing, the instructions include one selvage stitch at each side; these stitches are not included in the final measurements.

- To increase, use the M1 technique (page 151).

- For sweater assembly, refer to the illustration for square-indented sleeve construction on page 156.

SUGGESTED ALTERNATE COLORWAYS
Alternate Colorway 1, left: Cascade Yarns' *Greenland* in Brick #3512 (A), English Rose #3515 (B), and Cotton Candy #3514 (C)

Alternate Colorway 2, right: Magenta #3516 (A), Orange #3530 (B), and Maize #3531 (C); (4)

Back

With the smaller needles and A, cast on 59 (65, 71, 77) stitches.

Change to B, and work even in the Rib Pattern until the piece measures approximately 1½ (2, 2, 2)"/[4 (5, 5, 5)cm], ending after a wrong-side row.

Change to the larger needles and the Textured Stripe Pattern; work even until the piece measures approximately 8 (8½, 9, 9½)"/[20.5 (21.5, 23, 24)cm] from the beginning, ending after a wrong-side row.

SHAPE ARMHOLES

Bind off 6 (9, 9, 12) stitches at the beginning of the next 2 rows—47 (47, 53, 53) stitches remain.

Work even until the armholes measure approximately 5 (5½, 6, 6½)"/[12.5 (14, 15, 16.5)cm], ending after a wrong-side row.

SHAPE NECK

Next Row (RS): Work 13 (13, 15, 15) stitches; join a second ball of yarn and bind off the middle 21 (21, 23, 23) stitches, then work to the end of the row.

Decrease 1 stitch at the neck edge once—12 (12, 14, 14) stitches remain on each side.

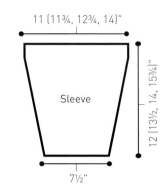

11 (11¾, 12¾, 14)"

Sleeve

12 (13½, 14, 15¾)"

7½"

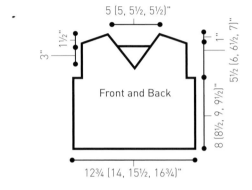

5 (5, 5½, 5½)"

1½"

3"

1"

5½ (6, 6½, 7)"

Front and Back

8 (8½, 9, 9½)"

12¾ (14, 15½, 16¾)"

Work even until the armholes measure approximately 5½ (6, 6½, 7)"/[14 (15, 16.5, 18)cm], ending after a wrong-side row.

SHAPE SHOULDERS

Bind off 3 (3, 4, 4) stitches at the beginning of the next 4 rows, then bind off 3 stitches at the beginning of the last 4 rows.

Front

Work the same as for the Back until the armholes measure approximately 2 (2½, 3, 3½)"/[5 (6.5, 7.5, 9)cm], ending after a wrong-side row.

SHAPE NECK

Decrease Row (RS): Work 20 (20, 23, 23) stitches, k2tog, place a marker, k1; join a second ball of yarn and bind off the middle stitch, k1, place a marker, ssk, work to the end of the row—22 (22, 25, 25) stitches remain on each side.

Decrease Row (WS): Slipping the markers, work to 2 stitches before the first marker, ssp, p1; with the second ball of yarn, p1, p2tog, work to the end of the row—21 (21, 24, 24) stitches remain on each side.

Repeat the last 2 rows 0 (0, 1, 1) more time, then decrease at the neck edges every right-side row 9 (9, 8, 8) times—12 (12, 14, 14) stitches remain on each side.

Work even on both sides at once with separate balls of yarn until the armholes measure the same as the Back to the shoulders.

SHAPE SHOULDERS
Work the same as for the Back.

Sleeves (Make 2)
With the smaller needles and A, cast on 35 stitches.

Change to B, and work even in the Rib Pattern until the piece measures approximately 1½ (2, 2, 2)"/[4 (5, 5, 5]cm], ending after a wrong-side row.

Change to the larger needles and the Textured Stripe Pattern; increase 1 stitch at each side every 4 rows 0 (0, 1, 8) time(s), every 6 rows 4 (6, 11, 7) times, then every 8 rows 4 (4, 0, 0) times, working new stitches into the pattern as they accumulate—51 (55, 59, 65) stitches.

Work even until the piece measures approximately 12 (13½, 14, 15¾)"/[30.5 (34.5, 35.5, 40)cm] from the beginning, ending after a wrong-side row.

Bind off.

Finishing
Weave in all remaining yarn tails.

Block the pieces to the finished measurements.

Sew the shoulder seams.

Textured Stripe Pattern
(mult 6 + 5 sts)

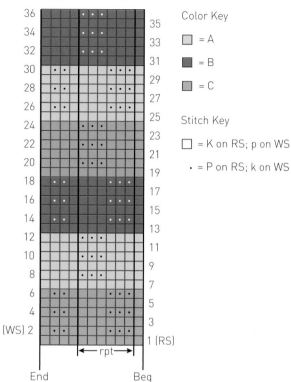

Color Key

□ = A

■ = B

▨ = C

Stitch Key

□ = K on RS; p on WS

• = P on RS; k on WS

← rpt →

End   Beg

NECKBAND
With the right side facing, using a circular needle and B, and beginning at the center front neck shaping, pick up and knit 87 (87, 89, 89) stitches evenly spaced along the neckline. *Do not join.*

Work even in the Rib Pattern until the band measures approximately ¾"/[2cm].

Next Row: Change to A, and work 1 row in the Rib Pattern.

Next Row: With A, bind off in the Rib Pattern.

With the right side overlapping the left side, sew the neckband edges into place.

Set in the Sleeves.

Sew the sleeve and side seams.

Joan's Hoodie

Practicing Basic Color Knitting Techniques

Simple stripes grace this comfy hoodie. Its fully fashioned shaping makes it particularly special. Don't tell anyone how easy it was to make—everyone will want one!

NOTES

- The instructions include one selvage stitch on each side; these stitches are not reflected in the finished measurements.

- For fully fashioned increases, use the M1-R and M1-L technique (page 151): K2, M1-R, work to the last 2 stitches, M1-L, k2.

- For fully fashioned decreases on right-side rows: K2, ssk, work to the last 4 stitches, k2tog, k2.

- For fully fashioned decreases on wrong-side rows: P2, p2tog, work to the last 4 stitches, ssp, p2.

- For sweater assembly, refer to the illustration for set-in sleeve construction on page 156.

SUGGESTED ALTERNATE COLORWAYS

Alternate Colorway 1, left: Trendsetter International's *M8* in White #100 (A), Blue #86277 (B), Bright Celery #9467 (C), and French Blue #6664 (D)

Alternate Colorway 2, right: Olive #8947 (A), Martini Olive #9963 (B), Lime #2062 (C), and Tarnished Gold #2066 (D); (**4**)

SKILL LEVEL

Easy

SIZES

S (M, L, 1X, 2X). Instructions are for the smallest size, with changes for the other sizes noted in parentheses as necessary.

FINISHED MEASUREMENTS

Bust (zipped): 35½ (39, 43½, 48¾, 52)"/ [90 (99, 110.5, 124, 132)cm]

Length: 21½ (22, 22½, 23, 23")/[54.5 (56, 57, 58.5, 58.5)cm]

MATERIALS

Trendsetter International's *M8*: 4-medium/worsted weight; 100% merino wool; each approximately 1¾ oz/[50g] and 100 yd/[91.5m]. 5 (6, 7, 8, 9) balls of Citrus #329 (A); 4 (5, 6, 7, 7) balls *each* of Tarnished Gold #2066 (B) and Cognac #9965 (C); and 2 (3, 3, 4, 4) balls of Butter #9940 (D); (**4**)

Size 7 (4.5mm) knitting needles

Size 8 (5mm) knitting needles, or size needed to obtain gauge

Size 8 (5mm) 32"/[80cm] circular needle, or size needed to obtain gauge

Two size 8 (5mm) double-pointed needles, or size needed to obtain gauge

Stitch markers

Two stitch holders

Blunt-end yarn needle

18 (18, 20, 20, 20)"/45.5 (45.5, 51, 51, 51) cm] separating zipper to match yarn

Sharp sewing needle

Thread to match zipper

(continued on next page.)

18 stitches and 26 rows = 4"/[10cm] in Stockinette Stitch with larger needles.

To save time, take time to check gauge.

STITCH PATTERNS

Seed Stitch (odd number of stitches)
Row 1 (RS): K1, *p1, k1; repeat from * across.

Repeat Row 1 for pattern.

*Stockinette Stitch
(any number of stitches)*
Row 1 (RS): Knit across.

Row 2: Purl across.

Repeat Rows 1 and 2 for the pattern.

Stripe Pattern
Work the 36-row Stripe Pattern in Stockinette Stitch as follows: *2 rows B, 2 rows C, 2 rows D, 2 rows A, 6 rows B, 2 rows C, 2 rows B, 2 rows A, 4 rows D, 2 rows B, 6 rows C, 4 rows A; repeat from * for the Stripe Pattern.

Back

With the smaller needles and A, cast on 81 (89, 99, 111, 119) stitches.

Work even in Seed Stitch until the piece measures approximately 1½"/[4cm], ending after a wrong-side row.

SET UP PATTERNS

Change to the larger needles; begin working the Stripe Pattern in Stockinette Stitch, and work even until the piece measures approximately 13"/[33cm], ending after a wrong-side row.

Make a note of which row of the Stripe Pattern you've ended with.

SHAPE ARMHOLES

Bind off 4 (5, 5, 6, 6) stitches at the beginning of the next 2 rows; bind off 2 (2, 3, 3, 4) stitches at the beginning of the following 2 rows—69 (75, 83, 93, 99) stitches remain.

Work fully fashioned decreases (Notes, page 69) at each side of every row 0 (2, 6, 10, 14) times, every other row 4 (4, 3, 4, 2) times, then every 4 rows 2 (2, 2, 1, 1) time(s)—57 (59, 61, 63, 65) stitches remain.

Work even until the armhole measures approximately 7½ (8, 8½, 9, 9)"/[19 (20.5, 21.5, 23, 23)cm] from the beginning.

SHAPE SHOULDERS

Bind off 5 (5, 5, 6, 6) stitches at the beginning of the next 4 rows, then bind off 4 (5, 6, 5, 6) stitches at the beginning of the next 2 rows—29 stitches remain.

Bind off. *Make a note of which color you used to bind off with.*

Left Front

With the smaller needles and A, cast on 41 (45, 51, 57, 61) stitches.

Work even in Seed Stitch until the piece measures approximately 1½"/[4cm], ending after a wrong-side row.

Pattern Set-Up Row (RS): Change to the larger needles; work the first 34 (38, 44, 50, 54) stitches in Stockinette

Stitch in the Stripe Pattern, place a marker; join a ball of A and work the last 7 stitches in Seed Stitch with A for the front band.

Work even in the established patterns until the piece measures the same as for the Back to the armhole, ending after the same row of the Stripe Pattern as you did for the Back to the armhole.

SHAPE ARMHOLE

Bind off 4 (5, 5, 6, 6) stitches at the armhole edge once, then bind off 2 (2, 3, 3, 4) stitches at the armhole edge once—35 (38, 43, 48, 51) stitches remain.

Work fully fashioned decreases (Notes, page 69) at the armhole edge every row 0 (2, 6, 10, 14) times, every other row 4 (4, 3, 4, 2) times, then every 4 rows 2 (2, 2, 1, 1) time(s)—29 (30, 32, 33, 34) stitches remain.

Work even until the armhole measures approximately 5 (5, 7, 7, 7)"/[12.5 (12.5, 18, 18, 18)cm], ending after a right-side row.

SHAPE NECK

Next Row (WS): Work the first 7 stitches and slip them onto a holder; continue across to the end of the row.

Bind off 3 (3, 4, 4, 4) stitches at the neck edge once, then decrease 1 stitch at the neck edge every row 3 times, then every other row twice—14 (15, 16, 17, 18) stitches remain.

Work even until the piece measures the same as for the Back to the shoulders, ending after a wrong-side row.

SHAPE SHOULDERS

Bind off 5 (5, 5, 6, 6) stitches at the armhole edge twice—4 (5, 6, 5, 6) stitches remain.

Work 1 row even.

Bind off.

Right Front

Work the same as for the Left Front *except* reverse the placement of the front band and reverse all shaping.

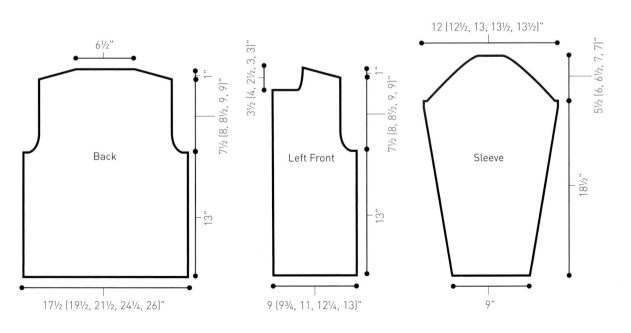

Sleeves (Make 2)

With the smaller needles and A, cast on 41 stitches.

Begin Seed Stitch, and work even until the piece measures approximately 1½"/[4cm], ending after a wrong-side row.

Change to the larger needles and B; begin Stockinette Stitch in the Stripe Pattern, and work fully fashioned increases (Notes, page 69) at each side of every 10 rows 0 (0, 2, 8, 8) times, every 12 rows 0 (4, 7, 2, 2) times, every 14 rows 4 (4, 0, 0, 0) times, then every 16 rows 3 (0, 0, 0, 0) times—55 (57, 59, 61, 61) stitches.

Work even until the piece measures approximately 18½"/[47cm], ending after the same row of the Stripe Pattern as you did for the Back.

SHAPE CAP

Bind off 4 (5, 5, 6, 6) stitches at the beginning of the next 2 rows, then work fully fashioned decreases (Notes, page 69) at each side of every 4 rows 1 (3, 4, 5, 5) time(s), then every other row 12 (10, 10, 9, 9) times—21 stitches remain.

Bind off 2 stitches at the beginning of the next 4 rows—13 stitches remain.

Bind off.

Finishing

Weave in all remaining yarn tails.

Block all pieces to the finished measurements.

Sew the shoulder seams.

HOOD

With the right side facing, using the larger needles and A, work in Seed Stitch as established across the 7 stitches from the Right Front neck holder, place a marker; using the same color you used to bind off the Back neck stitches, pick up and knit 61 stitches along the neckline, place a marker; with A, work in Seed Stitch as established across the 7 stitches from the Left Front neck holder—75 stitches total.

Continuing to work the first and last 7 stitches in Seed Stitch with A, work the remaining stitches in Stockinette Stitch in the established Stripe Pattern until the hood measures approximately 1"/[2.5cm], ending after a wrong-side row.

Next Row (RS): Continuing in the established patterns, work across 37 stitches, place a marker, k1, place a marker, work to the end of the row.

Next Row: Work even.

Next (Increase) Row: Work to the first marker, M1-L, slip the marker, k1, slip the marker, M1-R, work to the end of the row—77 stitches.

Repeat the Increase Row every 8 rows 6 more times—89 stitches.

Work even until the hood measures approximately 12½"/[32cm], ending after a right-side row.

Next Row: Work to the first marker; removing both markers, p2tog, eliminating the center stitch; work to the end of the row—88 stitches remain.

Divide the remaining stitches onto 2 double-pointed needles with 44 stitches on each needle; with the right side facing, graft the stitches together or bind them off and sew using mattress stitch seams (page 154).

Set in the Sleeves.

Sew the side and sleeve seams.

Weave in all remaining yarn tails.

Sew in the zipper.

Nubby Stripes Cardi

Creating Easy Vertical Stripes

I bet you'll knit this cute little number again and again. Made all in one piece from cuff to cuff, there's practically no finishing!

SKILL LEVEL
Easy

SIZES
Infant's 6 (12, 24) months. Instructions are for the smallest size, with changes for the other sizes noted in parentheses as necessary.

FINISHED MEASUREMENTS
Chest (buttoned): 21¼ (26, 28)"
/[54 (66, 71)cm]

Length: 11¾ (12½, 13¾)"
/[30 (32, 34.5)cm]

MATERIALS
Cascade Yarns' *Luna:* 4-medium/ worsted weight; 100% cotton; each approximately 1¾ oz/[21g] and 82 yd/ [75m]. 3 (3, 4) hanks *each* of Light Blue #725 (A) and Light Kiwi #728 (B), and 2 (2, 3) hanks of Light Yellow #724 (C); (4)

Size 6 (4mm) 24"/[60cm] circular needle

Size 7 (4.5mm) 24"/[60cm] circular needle, or size needed to obtain gauge

Stitch holders or waste yarn

One 1"/[2.5cm] button (JHB International's *Perforated Lime, Style #15905* was used on sample garment)

Blunt-end yarn needle

GAUGE
16 stitches and 28 rows = 4"/[10cm] in Seed Stitch using larger needle.

To save time, take time to check gauge.

STITCH PATTERN
Seed Stitch (odd number of stitches)
Pattern Row: K1, *p1, k1; repeat from * to end.

Stripe Pattern
Work the 8-row Stripe Pattern in Seed Stitch as follows: *2 rows A, 2 rows B, 2 rows C, 2 rows B; repeat from *, ending after working 2 rows A.

NOTES

- To decrease in pattern at the beginning of a row: If the first stitch on the left-hand needle is a knit stitch, then k2tog; if the first stitch on the left-hand needle is a purl stitch, then p2tog.

- To decrease in pattern at the end of the row: If the last stitch on the left-hand needle is a knit stitch, then ssk; if the last stitch on the left-hand needle is a purl stitch, then ssp.

- To increase stitches, use M1 knitwise or M1 purlwise technique (page 151) as necessary to maintain the Seed Stitch pattern.

- The row counts given in the pattern text are critical for ensuring that stripes line up on the Front and the Back.

SUGGESTED ALTERNATE COLORWAYS
Alternate Colorway 1, left: Cascade Yarns' *Luna* in Purple Passion #711 (A), Lilac #726 (B), and White #701 (C)

Alternate Colorway 2, right: Azure Blue #721 (A), Red #707 (B), and Gold #712 (C); (4)

First Sleeve

With the larger needle and A, cast on 29 (29, 31) stitches.

Begin the Stripe Pattern in Seed Stitch, marking the first row as a right-side row.

Increase 1 stitch at each side every 6 rows 1 (1, 0) time, then every 8 rows 4 (5, 6) times—39 (41, 43) stitches.

Work even in the established pattern until the sleeve measures approximately 6½ (7½, 8)"/[16.5 (19, 20.5)cm), ending after a wrong-side row—46 (52, 56) rows have been worked total.

Body

Maintaining the established Stripe Pattern, cast on 28 (30, 34) stitches (for Back and Left Front) at the beginning of the next 2 rows—95 (101, 111) stitches.

Work even until the piece measures approximately 10 (12, 12½)"/[25.5 (30.5, 32)cm), ending after a wrong-side row—70 (84, 88) rows have been worked total.

DIVIDE BACK AND LEFT FRONT

Next Row (RS): Continuing the established Stripe Pattern, work the first 47 (50, 55) stitches and slip them onto a holder or waste yarn for the back of the sweater, then work to the end of the row—48 (51, 56) stitches remain for the Left Front.

Next Row: Work across the 48 (51, 56) Front stitches, turn.

SHAPE NECK

Next Row (RS): Bind off the first 4 stitches—44 (47, 52) stitches remain.

Next Row: Work even.

Next Row: Decrease 1 stitch, then work to the end of the row—43 (46, 51) stitches remain.

Next Row: Work even.

Next Row: Decrease 1 stitch, then work to the end of the row—42 (45, 50) stitches remain.

Work 13 (15, 19) rows even, ending after 2 rows have been worked with A; the Left Front measures approximately 6¼ (7¾, 8¼)"/[16 (19.5, 21)cm)—44 (54, 58) total rows have been worked on the Left Front.

Bind off *loosely* in pattern.

Right Front

With A, cast on 42 (45, 50) stitches.

Work even in Seed Stitch in the Stripe Pattern for 4 (6, 8) rows.

Buttonhole Row (RS): Work 2 stitches, bind off 3 stitches, then work to the end of the row.

Next Row: Work in the established patterns, casting on 3 stitches over the bound-off stitches of the previous row.

Work even for 4 (6, 8) rows.

SHAPE NECK

Next Row (RS): Increase 1 stitch at the beginning of the row, then work to the end of the row—43 (46, 51) stitches.

Next Row (WS): Work even.

Next Row: Increase 1 stitch at the beginning of the row, then work to the end of the row—44 (47, 52) stitches.

Work even for 2 rows—15 (19, 23) rows have been worked on the Right Front.

Next Row (WS): Work across the row, then using the cable cast-on technique, cast on 4 stitches—48 (51, 56) stitches.

Slip the stitches onto a holder or waste yarn.

Back

Slip the 47 (50, 55) Back stitches from the holder onto the needle, ready to work a wrong-side row.

Maintaining the Stripe Pattern, join the yarn and work 25 (23, 31) rows in the established patterns, ending with the same colored stripe as on the Right Front.

JOIN RIGHT FRONT AND BACK

Next Row (RS): Work across the Back stitches, then, with the right side facing, work across the 48 (51, 56) stitches from the right front holder—95 (101, 111) stitches.

Work even for 25 (31, 31) rows—78 (90, 98) rows have been worked on the Back total.

Second Sleeve

Bind off 28 (30, 34) stitches at the beginning of the next 2 rows—39 (41, 43) stitches remain.

Work 8 (6, 8) rows even.

Decrease 1 stitch at each side on the next row, then every 8 rows 3 (4, 5) times, then every 6 rows 1 (1, 0) time—29 (29, 31) stitches remain.

Work even for 7 rows, ending after working 2 rows with A; the Sleeve measures approximately 6½ (7½, 8)"/[16.5 (19, 20.5)cm].

Bind off in pattern.

Finishing

Weave in all remaining yarn tails.

Block the piece to the finished measurements.

COLLAR

With the smaller circular needle and A, beginning and ending halfway into the straight section of the front neckline, pick up and knit 35 (35, 44) stitches along the neck opening.

Work even in Seed Stitch in the Stripe Pattern for 1"/[2.5cm].

Change to the larger circular needle; increase 1 stitch at each side every 4 rows 3 times, working the new stitches in Seed Stitch as they accumulate—41 (41, 50) stitches total.

Bind off in pattern.

Weave in all remaining yarn tails.

Sew the sleeve and side seams.

Fold the sleeve cuffs up as desired and tack into place.

Sew on the button opposite the buttonhole.

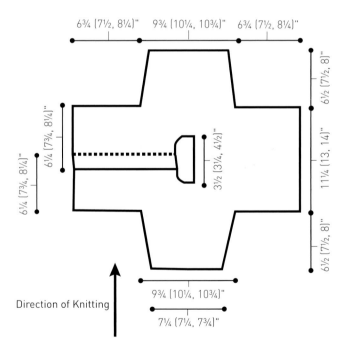

Mitered Mania Throw

Bending Stripes with Mitered Motifs

Here's a project that's perfect for knitters who don't like sewing seams. Each block is picked up and knitted directly onto previous ones.

SKILL LEVEL
Intermediate

SIZE
One size

FINISHED MEASUREMENTS
Approximately 51 x 66"/[129.5cm x 167.5cm], excluding edging

MATERIALS
Plymouth Yarn's *Encore Worsted*: 4-medium/worsted weight; 75% acrylic/25% wool; each approximately 3½ oz/[100g] and 200 yd/[183m]. 8 balls of Dark Forest Heather #670 (A), 4 balls of Light Forest Heather #678 (B), 6 balls of Taupe Heather #6003 (C), and 4 balls of Cream #1202 (D); (4)

Size 7 (4.5mm) knitting needles, or size needed to obtain gauge

Blunt-end yarn needle

GAUGE
Each rectangular motif measures 4¼"/ [11cm] wide x 2"/[5cm] high.

To save time, take time to check gauge.

STITCH PATTERN
Garter Stitch (any number of stitches)
Pattern Row: Knit across.

NOTES

- Always use the knit-on cast-on technique when casting on stitches.

- To increase stitches, use the M1-R and M1-L technique (page 151).

- To make picking up stitches easy, do a chain selvage as follows: Slip the first stitch of every row knitwise, and purl the last stitch of every row.

- For ease of finishing, after Motif 1, each motif is worked onto others. See page 48 for how to pick up and knit stitches for subsequent motifs.

- Weaving in ends as you go will greatly decrease the amount of finishing work after the throw is knit.

SUGGESTED ALTERNATE COLORWAYS
Alternate Colorway 1, left: Plymouth Yarn's *Encore Worsted* in Russet #212 (A), Harvest Gold #175 (B), Olive #045 (C), and Chocolate #599 (D)

Alternate Colorway 2, right: Creme #146 (A), Lavender #1033 (B), Light Lavender #233 (C), and Purple Magic #1034 (D); (4)

First Row of Motifs

MOTIF 1

With A, cast on 34 stitches (Notes, page 79).

Row 1 and all WS rows to last row: Sl 1 to begin chain selvage (Notes, page 79), knit to the last stitch, p1.

Row 2 (RS): Sl 1, k6, s2kp2, k14, s2kp2, k6, p1—30 stitches remain.

Row 4: Change to B; sl 1, k5, s2kp2, k12, s2kp2, k5, p1—26 stitches remain.

Row 6: Change to A; sl 1, k4, s2kp2, k10, s2kp2, k4, p1—22 stitches remain.

Row 8: Change to B; sl 1, k3, s2kp2, k8, s2kp2, k3, p1—18 stitches remain.

Row 10: Change to A; sl 1, k2, s2kp2, k6, s2kp2, k2, p1—14 stitches remain.

Row 12: Change to B; sl 1, k1, s2kp2, k4, s2kp2, k1, p1—10 stitches remain.

Row 14: Change to A; sl 1, s2kp2, k2, s2kp2, p1—6 stitches remain.

Row 16: S2kp2, s2kp2—2 stitches remain.

Row 17: K2tog—1 stitch remains.

Fasten off.

MOTIF 2

With C, cast on 25 stitches, then with the right side of Motif 1 facing, pick up and knit 9 stitches along the right-hand side of Motif 1—34 stitches.

Complete the same as for Motif 1 in the following color sequence:

Rows 1–3: Use C.

Rows 4 and 5: Use D.

Rows 6 and 7: Use C.

Rows 8 and 9: Use D.

Rows 10 and 11: Use C.

Rows 12 and 13: Use D.

Rows 14–17: Use C.

MOTIF 3

With A, cast on 25 stitches, then with the right side of Motif 2 facing, pick up and knit 9 stitches along the right-hand side of Motif 2—34 stitches.

Complete the same as for Motif 1.

MOTIFS 4, 6, 8, 10, AND 12

Work the same as for Motif 2, picking up stitches along the motif just worked.

MOTIFS 5, 7, 9, AND 11

Work the same as for Motif 3, picking up stitches along the motif just worked.

Second Row of Motifs

MOTIF 13

With the right side facing and C, pick up and knit 8 stitches along the top edge of Motif 12, then cast on 9 stitches—17 stitches.

Row 1 and all WS rows: Sl 1, knit to the last stitch, p1.

Row 2 (RS): Sl 1, k6, s2kp2, k6, p1—15 stitches remain.

Row 4: Change to D; sl 1, k5, s2kp2, k5, p1—13 stitches remain.

Row 6: Change to C; sl 1, k4, s2kp2, k4, p1—11 stitches remain.

Row 8: Change to D; sl 1, k3, s2kp2, k3, p1—9 stitches remain.

Row 10: Change to C; sl 1, k2, s2kp2, k2, p1—7 stitches remain.

Row 12: Change to D; sl 1, k1, s2kp2, k1, p1—5 stitches remain.

Row 14: Change to C; sl 1, s2kp2, p1—3 stitches remain.

Row 16: S2kp2—1 stitch remains.

Fasten off.

MOTIF 14

With the right side facing and A, pick up and knit 9 stitches along the left-hand edge of Motif 13, then pick up and knit 16 stitches along the top edge of Motifs 12 and 11, then cast on 9 stitches—34 stitches.

Complete the same as for Motif 1.

MOTIF 15

With the right side facing and C, pick up and knit 9 stitches along the left-hand edge of Motif 14, pick up and knit 16 stitches along the top edge of Motifs 11 and 10, then cast on 9 stitches—34 stitches.

Complete the same as for Motif 2.

Refer to the Construction Diagram on page 83 and complete Motifs 16–24, alternating the colors as shown in the photograph below.

MOTIF 25

With the right side facing and C, pick up and knit 9 stitches along the left-hand edge of Motif 24, then pick up and knit 8 stitches along the top edge of Motif 1—17 stitches.

Complete the same as for Motif 13.

Third Row of Motifs

MOTIF 26

With the right side facing and A, cast on 9 stitches, then pick up and knit 16 stitches along the top edges of Motifs 13 and 14, then cast on 9 stitches—34 stitches.

Complete the same as for Motif 1.

MOTIF 27

With the right side facing and C, cast on 9 stitches, then pick up and knit 16 stitches along the top edges of Motifs 14 and 15, then cast on 9 stitches—34 stitches.

Complete the same as for Motif 2.

Refer to the Construction Diagram and complete the Third Row of Motifs, alternating the colors as shown in the photograph, page 81.

Fourth Row of Motifs

MOTIF 38

With the right side facing and A, pick up and knit 8 stitches along the top edge of Motif 26, then cast on 9 stitches—17 stitches.

Refer to the Construction Diagram and complete the Fourth Row of Motifs, alternating the colors as shown in the photograph, page 81.

Remaining Rows of Motifs

Refer to the Construction Diagram and complete the Remaining Rows of Motifs, alternating the colors as shown in the photograph, page 81.

Finishing

BORDER

With the right side facing and A, pick up and knit 8 stitches in each motif along one long side of the throw—264 stitches.

Work 16 rows in Garter Stitch, and *at the same time* increase 1 stitch at the beginning and end of every right-side row as follows: K1, M1-R, knit to the last stitch, M1-L, k1—280 stitches when all increases are complete.

Bind off *loosely* as you purl on the wrong side.

Repeat the border along the opposite long side.

With the right side facing and A, pick up and knit 16 stitches in each motif along one short side of the throw—192 stitches.

Work 16 rows in Garter Stitch, and *at the same time* increase 1 stitch at the beginning and end of every right-side row as follows: K1, M1-R, knit to the last stitch, M1-L, k1—208 stitches when all increases are complete.

Bind off *loosely* as you purl on the wrong side.

Repeat the border along the opposite short side.

Use the invisible seaming method to sew corner seams, (page 155).

Weave in all remaining yarn tails.

Block to the finished measurements.

Construction Diagram

412	411	410	409	408	407	406	405	404	403	402	401	
400	399	398	397	396	395	394	393	392	391	390	389	388
387	386	385	384	383	382	381	380	379	378	377	376	
375	374	373	372	371	370	369	368	367	366	365	364	363
362	361	360	359	358	357	356	355	354	353	352	351	
350	349	348	347	346	345	344	343	342	341	340	339	338
337	336	335	334	333	332	331	330	329	328	327	326	
325	324	323	322	321	320	319	318	317	316	315	314	313
312	311	310	309	308	307	306	305	304	303	302	301	
300	299	298	297	296	295	294	293	292	291	290	289	288
287	286	285	284	283	282	281	280	279	278	277	276	
275	274	273	272	271	270	269	268	267	266	265	264	263
262	261	260	259	258	257	256	255	254	253	252	251	
250	249	248	247	246	245	244	243	242	241	240	239	238
237	236	235	234	233	232	231	230	229	228	227	226	
225	224	223	222	221	220	219	218	217	216	215	214	213
212	211	210	209	208	207	206	205	204	203	202	201	
200	199	198	197	196	195	194	193	192	191	190	189	188
187	186	185	184	183	182	181	180	179	178	177	176	
175	174	173	172	171	170	169	168	167	166	165	164	163
162	161	160	159	158	157	156	155	154	153	152	151	
150	149	148	147	146	145	144	143	142	141	140	139	138
137	136	135	134	133	132	131	130	129	128	127	126	
125	124	123	122	121	120	119	118	117	116	115	114	113
112	111	110	109	108	107	106	105	104	103	102	101	
100	99	98	97	96	95	94	93	92	91	90	89	88
87	86	85	84	83	82	81	80	79	78	77	76	
75	74	73	72	71	70	69	68	67	66	65	64	63
62	61	60	59	58	57	56	55	54	53	52	51	
50	49	48	47	46	45	44	43	42	41	40	39	38
37	36	35	34	33	32	31	30	29	28	27	26	
25	24	23	22	21	20	19	18	17	16	15	14	13
1	2	3	4	5	6	7	8	9	10	11	12	

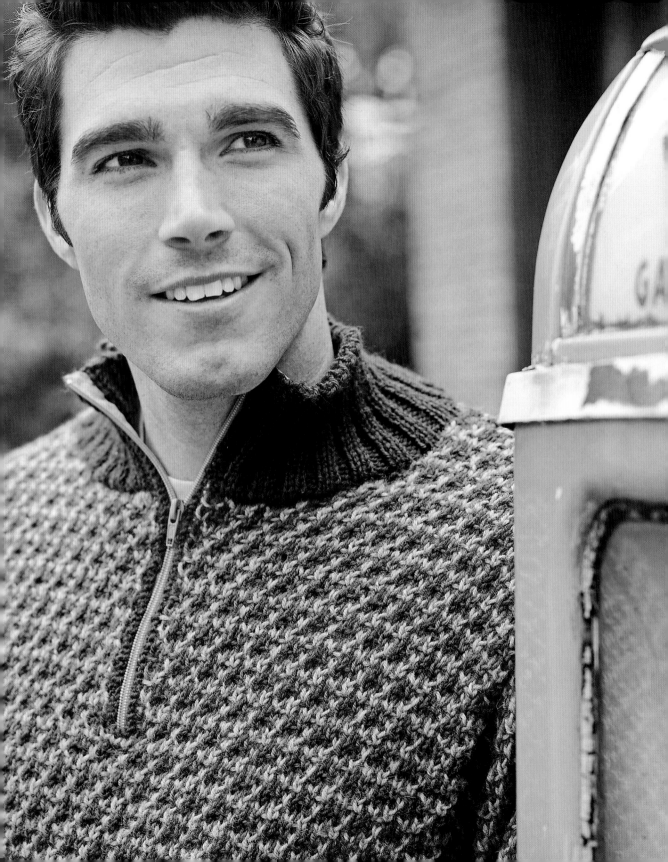

3 Creating Color Patterns
Using Slip Stitches

A subset of stripes, colorful slip stitch patterns are deceptively easy to knit. When slipping stitches from the left-hand needle to the right-hand one, you're simply moving them from one spot to another without working them. This maneuver elongates the stitch, drawing it up lengthwise, and when stripes are involved, gives the appearance of a second color yarn in a row of knitting that's worked with only one. It's two-color knitting the easy way!

Slip Stitch Techniques

The convention in knitting is always to slip stitches *purlwise* unless told otherwise. This ensures that the slipped stitch will be sitting on the needle in the desired orientation when it's time to work it. Of course, stitches can be slipped knitwise; however, usually that's done only when they're part of a decrease such as ssk or s2kp2. Following are the basics of slip stitch knitting, including how to move stitches from one needle to the other and where to hold the working yarn while doing so.

Charts for this type of knitting are used in the same manner as charts for simple stripes. Colored boxes indicate different colors of yarn, and here, symbols that look like Vs represent the stitches to be slipped. Plain Vs tell you to slip stitches with the working yarn in back, toward the *wrong side* of the fabric, and Vs with horizontal dashes across them mean you'll slip stitches with the working yarn in front, on the *right side*. For garter stitch fabrics, tiny dots inside the boxes will remind you to purl the stitches on right-side rows and knit them on wrong-side rows.

Slip stitch patterns easily lend themselves to graphic designs. Whether you are creating a honeycomb, plaid, or windowpane design, or even an Op Art masterpiece (page 134), charts will allow you to take in the overall design quickly. At first glance, in the Pattern Treasury of Slip Stitches, for example, Slip Stitch Pattern 25 (page 107) looks like a woman dancing—and you haven't even begun knitting it yet! And Slip Stitch Pattern 21 (page 105) is easily recognized as a Greek Key motif. Slip stitch patterns are some of the most fun to chart out. Grab some graph paper and give it a whirl!

Placement of Working Yarn

The position of the working yarn is important when slipping stitches, and knitting patterns will indicate whether the yarn should be held in the front or the back of the fabric. Carrying the yarn along the wrong side of the fabric allows the slipped stitches from the previous row to show in their entirety, while holding the yarn toward the right side of the fabric creates a pattern of contrasting, textured blips.

Slipping Stitches with Yarn in Back

When instructed to hold the yarn in back, slip the stitch onto the right-hand needle purlwise, keeping the working yarn behind the fabric as it faces you (illustration 1).

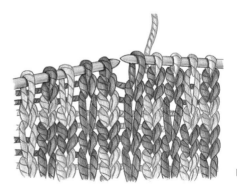

[1]

Slipping Stitches with Yarn in Front

To slip a stitch with the yarn in front, bring the working yarn to the front of the fabric (such as when purling) and slip the stitch (illustration 2). When moving the yarn *from front to back* or from back to front, be careful always to bring it *between the tips* of the knitting needles and not over the right-hand needle. Otherwise, you will create a yarn over that will increase your stitch count and make an unexpected hole in your fabric.

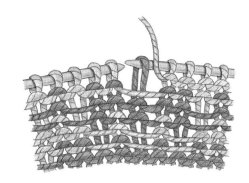

[2]

Texture within Slip Stitch Fabrics

When you begin knitting slip stitch patterns, you'll notice that texture plays a big part in the finished look. Knitters have the choice of many surface textures within these patterns. At times it seems as though there are as many textures as there are possible stitch combinations! With so many options available to us, it can help to think about slip stitch texture as both fabric-based and float-based.

When categorizing these patterns according to their base fabrics, simply changing the fabric from stockinette to garter—or sometimes even using a combination of both—completely alters the look. For example, slipping stitches within solid stockinette stitch creates a smooth fabric, but slipping stitches within garter stitch yields a nubby fabric. To highlight the textural possibilities caused by different base fabrics, we'll begin by using the same basic design in this section and knit it in three different base fabrics: stockinette, garter, and a combination of the two. It's astonishing to see how the same chart looks so different in each one. Best of all, you can work nearly any slip stitch or mosaic stitch chart using these textures.

We can also categorize slip stitch fabrics according to where the yarn is held while slipping stitches: Usually, the working yarn is carried on the wrong side of the fabric, but sometimes it is deliberately carried along the public side. With this slight (and easy) change in technique, horizontal "floats," or strands, of yarn are visible and become an important part of the pattern design. Like the various fabric-based variations, this type of slip stitch pattern offers myriad options. Some designs even use simple knitting gymnastics—easy ones, I promise—to manipulate those horizontal strands of yarn in unexpected and visually exciting ways. Whatever texture you choose, you'll dramatically change the look of easy one-color-per-row knitting with merely a simple slip of the stitch.

Stockinette Stitch–Based Fabric

The simplest slip stitch patterns have a stockinette stitch base for the fabric: On right-side rows, stitches are either knitted or slipped with the yarn toward the back of the fabric; on wrong-side rows, stitches are purled or slipped with the yarn toward you. All stitches—those in the background as well as the contrasting patterned ones—are smooth like stockinette stitch, and all the horizontal floats are hidden on the non-public side of the fabric.

You'll probably find stockinette stitch–based fabrics the quickest slip stitch variations to knit

because the yarn never has to be moved to the front or the back between stitches. On right-side rows, the yarn stays in the back of the fabric (away from you) whether you're knitting or slipping a stitch; on wrong-side rows, the yarn stays to the front at all times.

Although stockinette stitch–based slip stitch patterns are not difficult to work up, they often amaze nonknitters. They'll think you've used two colors in each row. The following chart shows how easily this trick is accomplished. Notice how the slipped stitches, represented by Vs in the chart, bring the colors of the previous rows up into successive rows. Only a fellow knitter would guess that one color was worked at a time!

SLIP STITCH PATTERN IN STOCKINETTE STITCH

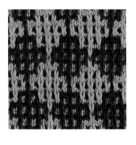

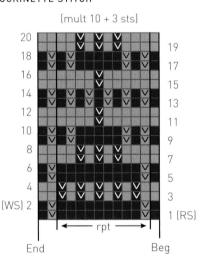

(mult 10 + 3 sts)

To begin: CO with B and purl 1 row.

Color Key

■ = A

▨ = B

Stitch Key

☐ = K on RS; p on WS

∨ = Slip st purlwise with yarn in back on RS rows; slip st purlwise with yarn in front on WS rows

Garter Stitch–Based Fabric

The same slip stitch pattern can be worked in garter stitch. In this case, all stitches that are worked on wrong-side rows are knitted (not purled), and the yarn is brought back to the wrong side as you slip the other stitches. The resulting fabric is noncurling and flat, ideal for afghans and throws. Again, all horizontal floats are hidden on the wrong-side of the fabric.

SLIP STITCH PATTERN IN GARTER STITCH

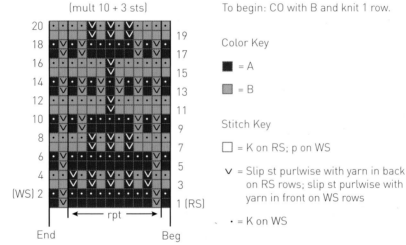

(mult 10 + 3 sts)

(WS) 2 · · · 1 (RS)

End

Beg

rpt

To begin: CO with B and knit 1 row.

Color Key

■ = A

▦ = B

Stitch Key

☐ = K on RS; p on WS

V = Slip st purlwise with yarn in back on RS rows; slip st purlwise with yarn in front on WS rows

· = K on WS

color PLAY

In these garter stitch–based fabrics or in any slip stitch pattern in which stitches are both slipped with the yarn in front as well as knitted, it is extremely common to inadvertently create yarn overs on wrong-side rows. (And, as any beginner knitter will tell you happily, these yarn overs will increase your stitch count and make great big holes in your fabric!) To prevent this issue, be sure to bring the working yarn between the needle tips (and not over the right-hand needle) before each slipped stitch and then back again prior to knitting the next stitch when working wrong-side rows.

Right: The Everyday Clutch, page 120, showcases a slip stitch pattern worked in highly textured stockinette–and garter stitch–based fabric.

Combined Stockinette– and Garter Stitch–Based Fabric

For more contrast in texture, you can place textured garter stitch–based slip stitch patterns on smooth stockinette stitch grounds to create very successful designs. Here's our same slip stitch pattern chart using a combination of stitches: The base fabric is stockinette stitch, and the contrasting pattern stitches are garter stitch ridges. Worked this way, the contrast color really "pops" on the smooth background. And, since the horizontal floats are all hidden on the wrong side of the fabric, the pattern appears crisp and well defined.

SLIP STITCH PATTERN WITH GARTER RIDGES

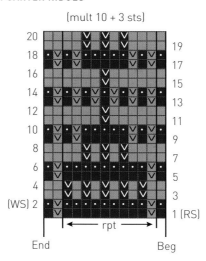

(mult 10 + 3 sts)

rpt

End

Beg

To begin: CO with B and purl 1 row

Color Key

■ = A

▨ = B

Stitch Key

□ = K on RS; p on WS

∨ = Slip st purlwise with yarn in back on RS rows; slip st purlwise with yarn in front on WS rows

• = K on WS

Linen Stitch Fabric

Here's a beautiful and useful slip stitch pattern that deliberately showcases its horizontal floats of yarn on the public side of the fabric, creating a colorful, textured pattern. Like many other fabrics made with this technique, linen stitch resembles a woven tweedy fabric.

As you can see in the following chart, the slipped stitches in this linen stitch swatch are indicated by Vs (the slip stitches) slashed with horizontal lines. These dashes through the stitches represent the floats of yarn that will be visible on the public side of the fabric. When you're on a right-side row, carry the working yarn toward you as you slip stitches; on wrong-side rows, strand it behind the slipped stitches.

Other examples of float-based fabrics (made with stitches slipped with the working yarn in front) can be found in the Pattern Treasury of Slip Stitches, such as Slip Stitch Pattern 39 (page 115).

color **PLAY**

Mosaic pattern stitches are a subset of slip stitch patterns. Developed by Barbara G. Walker, these designs can be worked using any of the stockinette stitch and garter stitch textures already mentioned in this section. Her mosaic charts are half the height, since wrong-side rows are not shown. For wrong-side rows, the pattern of working and slipping stitches is repeated from the previous row.

LINEN STITCH PATTERN

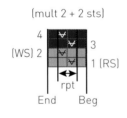

(mult 2 + 2 sts)

To begin: CO with A and purl 1 row.

Color Key

■ = A

▨ = B

Stitch Key

☐ = K on RS; p on WS

⋎ = Slip st purlwise with yarn in front on RS rows; slip st purlwise with yarn in back on WS rows

Fabrics with Manipulated Floats

Slipping several adjacent stitches with the working yarn held in front, toward the right side of the fabric, creates extremely long horizontal floats. On subsequent rows, these exaggerated floats can be picked up to create beautiful, textured effects. The manipulated strands create a quilted effect in a piece of fabric knitted this way.

It's easy to do this technique: simply insert your right-hand needle under the floating strands, being sure to catch all of them at once without piercing the fabric behind them, and then work the next stitch, catching the extra strands inside (illustration 3).

[3]

The chart for this type of slip stitch pattern is simple to use. Notice that the symbol for drawing up the strands (in Rows 5 and 11) is centrally located above the slipped stitches several rows below. When pulled up, the horizontal strands of yarn that were floating in front of those slipped stitches create zigzag lines on top of the fabric.

MANIPULATING FLOATING STRANDS PATTERN

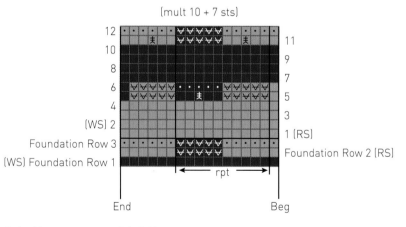

(mult 10 + 7 sts)

rpt

End

Beg

Color Key

■ = A

■ = B

Stitch Key

□ = K on RS; p on WS

⅄ = Slip st purlwise with yarn in front on RS rows; slip st purlwise with yarn in back on WS rows

• = K on WS

⅄ = Insert RH needle under the 2 loose strands several rows below and knit next st, catching strands

Designer's Workshop: Designing with Slip Stitches

It's fun to design original knitting patterns using slipped stitches. Get out some graph paper or your favorite charting program (such as Design-a-Knit by Softbyte) and have a go at it!

• Try using slipped stitches to draw outlines of shapes or for plaids and windowpanes. Charts make it easy for you to visualize your knitted fabric before you pick up your needles!

• To chart out your own slip stitch patterns by hand, start by drawing two-row horizontal stripes of alternating colors, then add short vertical lines to indicate the slipped stitches.

• Once you've drawn a chart you like, try knitting it in different textures. Garter stitch ridges on wrong-side rows add drama with very little effort!

• When designing fabrics with manipulated strands of yarn, be sure the floating strands are wide enough to be pulled up the desired height. If they're too short, the fabric will pucker. Be sure to knit a swatch to check.

• If floating strands are not going to be pulled up on subsequent rows, only place two or three slipped stitches adjacent to one another—otherwise the fabric might get distorted. Of course, such puckering can be used as a design element if desired.

• Try cabling the elongated slipped stitches on subsequent rows. Slip Stitch Pattern 45 (page 118) uses this interesting technique.

• Create complexity without much effort by using a variegated or hand-painted yarn as one of the colors. The Everyday Clutch (page 120) has solid-colored textured pattern stitches sitting on a smooth multicolor ground.

• There's no reason why both the background and contrast yarns must be the same material! Try using a fuzzy mohair or chenille with a smooth wool. As always, be certain that every yarn used within a project has the same laundering instructions.

• You can create a complex color pattern within a slip stitch pattern as I have in Cleo's Jacket (page 136). If you're designing a garment, you'll probably want to place the darkest colors toward the bottom and the lightest colors toward the top. This designer trick draws the eye up toward the wearer's face, creating more flattering sweaters, especially for pear-shaped or petite body frames.

Pattern Treasury of Slip Stitches

Here's a collection of slip stitch patterns for you to use in your knitting projects. Notice that slipped stitches are a great way to work stripes that don't look at all stripy. Plus, they appear so much more complicated than they really are! Each pattern includes a chart and sample swatch so that you can easily find the perfect patterns for your projects. If you need a quick refresher course on chart reading or suggestions on how best to use this pattern treasury, turn to pages 144 and 149.

Once you've played around with these stitch patterns, I hope you'll experiment and come up with your own. The possibilities are nearly endless!

SLIP STITCH PATTERN 1

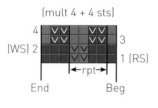

(mult 4 + 4 sts)

To begin: CO with B and purl 1 row.

Color Key

■ = A

■ = B

Stitch Key

□ = K on RS; p on WS

∨ = Slip st purlwise with yarn in back on RS rows; slip st purlwise with yarn in front on WS rows

---

SLIP STITCH PATTERN 2

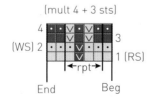

(mult 4 + 3 sts)

To begin: CO with A and knit 1 row.

Color Key

■ = A

□ = B

Stitch Key

□ = K on RS; p on WS

· = K on WS

∨ = Slip st purlwise with yarn in back on RS rows; slip st purlwise with yarn in front on WS rows

SLIP STITCH PATTERN 3

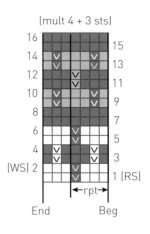

(mult 4 + 3 sts)

To begin: CO with B and purl 1 row.

Color Key

□ = A

■ = B

■ = C

Stitch Key

□ = K on RS; p on WS

∨ = Slip st purlwise with yarn in back on RS rows; slip st purlwise with yarn in front on WS rows

SLIP STITCH PATTERN 4

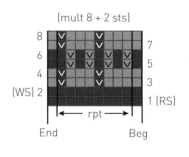

(mult 8 + 2 sts)

To begin: CO with B and purl 1 row.

Color Key

■ = A

■ = B

Stitch Key

□ = K on RS; p on WS

∨ = Slip st purlwise with yarn in back on RS rows; slip st purlwise with yarn in front on WS rows

SLIP STITCH PATTERN 5

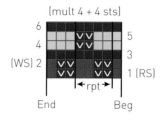

(mult 4 + 4 sts)

To begin: CO with C and purl 1 row.

Color Key

☐ = A

■ = B

■ = C

Stitch Key

☐ = K on RS; p on WS

∨ = Slip st purlwise with yarn
   in back on RS rows; slip st
   purlwise with yarn in front
   on WS rows

SLIP STITCH PATTERN 6

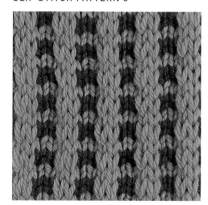

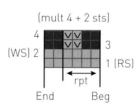

(mult 4 + 2 sts)

To begin: CO with B and purl 1 row.

Color Key

■ = A

■ = B

Stitch Key

☐ = K on RS; p on WS

∨ = Slip st purlwise with yarn
   in back on RS rows; slip st
   purlwise with yarn in front
   on WS rows

SLIP STITCH PATTERN 7

(mult 6 + 5 sts)

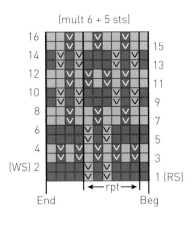

End   Beg

←rpt→

To begin: CO with B
and purl 1 row.

Color Key

■ = A

■ = B

Stitch Key

□ = K on RS; p on WS

∨ = Slip st purlwise with
yarn in back on RS rows;
slip st purlwise with
yarn in front on WS rows

SLIP STITCH PATTERN 8

(mult 4 + 2 sts)

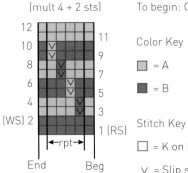

End   Beg

←rpt→

To begin: CO with A and purl 1 row.

Color Key

■ = A

■ = B

Stitch Key

□ = K on RS; p on WS

∨ = Slip st purlwise with yarn in back
on RS rows; slip st purlwise with
yarn in front on WS rows

SLIP STITCH PATTERN 9

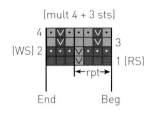

(mult 4 + 3 sts)

To begin: CO with B and knit 1 row.

Color Key

■ = A

■ = B

Stitch Key

□ = K on RS; p on WS

• = P on RS; k on WS

∨ = Slip st purlwise with yarn
in back on RS rows; slip st
purlwise with yarn in front
on WS rows

SLIP STITCH PATTERN 10

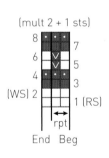

(mult 2 + 1 sts)

To begin: CO with B and knit 1 row.

Color Key

□ = A

■ = B

Stitch Key

□ = K on RS; p on WS

• = P on RS; k on WS

∨ = Slip st purlwise with yarn in back on
RS rows; slip st purlwise with yarn
in front on WS rows

SLIP STITCH PATTERN 11

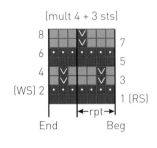

(mult 4 + 3 sts)

←rpt→

End   Beg

To begin: CO with B and purl 1 row.

Color Key

■ = A

■ = B

Stitch Key

□ = K on RS; p on WS

• = P on RS; k on WS

∨ = Slip st purlwise with yarn
in back on RS rows; slip st
purlwise with yarn in front
on WS rows

SLIP STITCH PATTERN 12

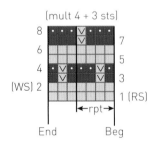

(mult 4 + 3 sts)

←rpt→

End   Beg

To begin: CO with B and knit 1 row.

Color Key

□ = A

■ = B

Stitch Key

□ = K on RS; p on WS

• = P on RS; k on WS

∨ = Slip st purlwise with yarn
in back on RS rows; slip st
purlwise with yarn in front
on WS rows

SLIP STITCH PATTERN 13

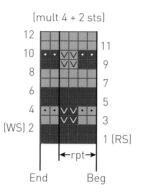

(mult 4 + 2 sts)

12
10
8
6
4
(WS) 2

11
9
7
5
3
1 (RS)

←rpt→

End   Beg

To begin: CO with B and purl 1 row.

Color Key

■ = A

■ = B

Stitch Key

□ = K on RS; p on WS

• = P on RS; k on WS

V = Slip st purlwise with yarn
in back on RS rows; slip st
purlwise with yarn in front
on WS rows

SLIP STITCH PATTERN 14

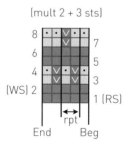

(mult 2 + 3 sts)

8
6
4
(WS) 2

7
5
3
1 (RS)

←rpt→

End   Beg

To begin: CO with B and knit 1 row.

Color Key

■ = A

□ = B

Stitch Key

□ = K on RS; p on WS

• = P on RS; k on WS

V = Slip st purlwise with yarn in back
on RS rows; slip st purlwise with
yarn in front on WS rows

SLIP STITCH PATTERN 15

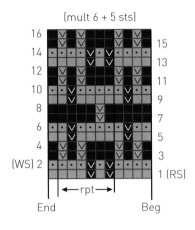

(mult 6 + 5 sts)

To begin: CO with B and purl 1 row.

Color Key

▨ = A

■ = B

Stitch Key

☐ = K on RS; p on WS

• = P on RS; k on WS

∨ = Slip st purlwise with
yarn in back on RS rows;
slip st purlwise with yarn
in front on WS rows

SLIP STITCH PATTERN 16

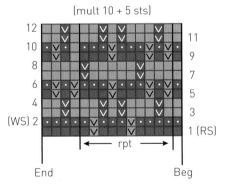

(mult 10 + 5 sts)

To begin: CO with B and purl 1 row.

Color Key

■ = A

▨ = B

Stitch Key

☐ = K on RS; p on WS

• = K on WS

∨ = Slip st purlwise with yarn in back on RS rows;
slip st purlwise with yarn in front on WS rows

SLIP STITCH PATTERN 17

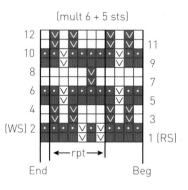

(mult 6 + 5 sts)

To begin: CO with B and purl 1 row.

Color Key

■ = A

□ = B

Stitch Key

□ = K on RS; p on WS

· = K on WS

∨ = Slip st purlwise with yarn in back on RS rows; slip st purlwise with yarn in front on WS rows

---

SLIP STITCH PATTERN 18

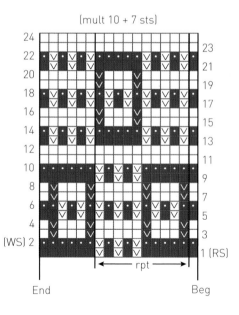

(mult 10 + 7 sts)

To begin: CO with B and purl 1 row.

Color Key   Stitch Key

■ = A   □ = K on RS; p on WS

□ = B   · = K on WS

∨ = Slip st purlwise with yarn in back on RS rows; slip st purlwise with yarn in front on WS rows

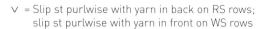

SLIP STITCH PATTERN 19

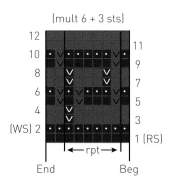

(mult 6 + 3 sts)

To begin: CO with B and purl 1 row.

Color Key

■ = A

■ = B

Stitch Key

□ = K on RS; p on WS

• = K on WS

∨ = Slip st purlwise with yarn in back on RS rows; slip st purlwise with yarn in front on WS rows

---

SLIP STITCH PATTERN 20

To begin: CO with B and purl 1 row.

Color Key   Stitch Key

■ = A   □ = K on RS; p on WS

■ = B   • = K on WS

∨ = Slip st purlwise with yarn in back on RS rows; slip st purlwise with yarn in front on WS rows

(mult 12 + 3 sts)

SLIP STITCH PATTERN 21

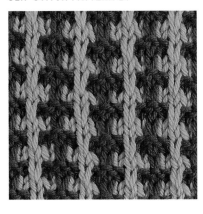

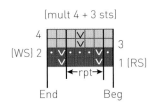

To begin: CO with A and purl 1 row.

Color Key

■ = A

■ = B

Stitch Key

□ = K on RS; p on WS

• = K on WS

∨ = Slip st purlwise with yarn in back on RS rows; slip st purlwise with yarn in front on WS rows

SLIP STITCH PATTERN 22

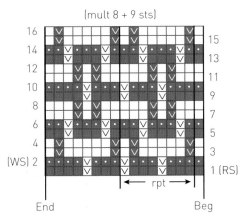

To begin: CO with B and purl 1 row.

Color Key

■ = A

□ = B

Stitch Key

□ = K on RS; p on WS

• = P on RS; k on WS

∨ = Slip st purlwise with yarn in back on RS rows; slip st purlwise with yarn in front on WS rows

SLIP STITCH PATTERN 23

(mult 12 + 3 sts)

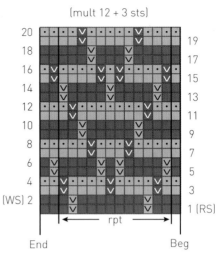

To begin: CO with B and knit 1 row.

Color Key

■ = A

■ = B

Stitch Key

□ = K on RS; p on WS

• = K on WS

∨ = Slip st purlwise with yarn in back on RS rows; slip st purlwise with yarn in front on WS rows

---

SLIP STITCH PATTERN 24

(mult 12 + 3 sts)

To begin: CO with B and purl 1 row.

Color Key

■ = A

■ = B

Stitch Key

□ = K on RS; p on WS

• = K on WS

∨ = Slip st purlwise with yarn in back on RS rows; slip st purlwise with yarn in front on WS rows

SLIP STITCH PATTERN 25

(mult 12 + 3 sts)

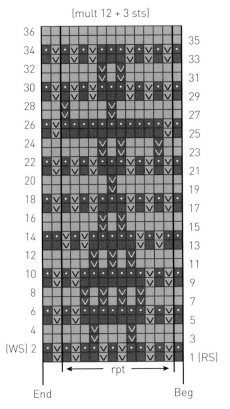

To begin: CO with B and purl 1 row.

Color Key

■ = A

▨ = B

Stitch Key

□ = K on RS; p on WS

· = K on WS

v = Slip st purlwise with yarn in back on RS rows;
slip st purlwise with yarn in front on WS rows

SLIP STITCH PATTERN 26

(mult 14 + 3 sts)

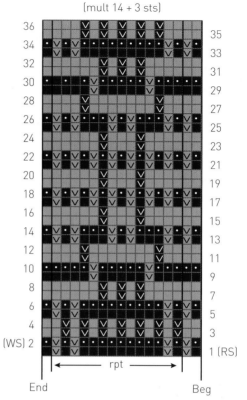

To begin: CO with B and purl 1 row.

Color Key

■ = A

■ = B

Stitch Key

☐ = K on RS; p on WS

· = K on WS

∨ = Slip st purlwise with yarn in back on RS rows;
slip st purlwise with yarn in front on WS rows

SLIP STITCH PATTERN 27

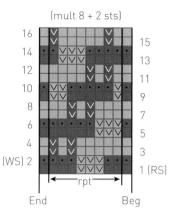

(mult 8 + 2 sts)

End   Beg

To begin: CO with B and purl 1 row.

Color Key

■ = A

□ = B

Stitch Key

□ = K on RS; p on WS

· = K on WS

∨ = Slip st purlwise with yarn in back on RS rows; slip st purlwise with yarn in front on WS rows

SLIP STITCH PATTERN 28

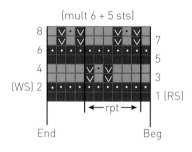

(mult 6 + 5 sts)

End   Beg

To begin: CO with B and purl 1 row.

Color Key

■ = A

■ = B

Stitch Key

□ = K on RS; p on WS

· = P on RS; k on WS

∨ = Slip st purlwise with yarn in back on RS rows; slip st purlwise with yarn in front on WS rows

SLIP STITCH PATTERN 29

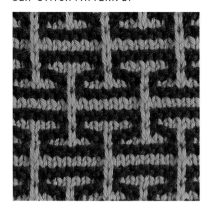

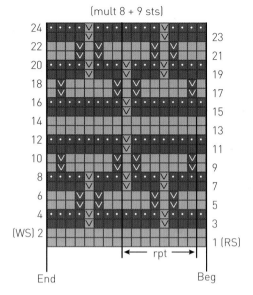

(mult 8 + 9 sts)

To begin: CO with A and knit 1 row.

Color Key

■ = A

■ = B

Stitch Key

□ = K on RS; p on WS

• = K on WS

∨ = Slip st purlwise with yarn in back on RS rows; slip st purlwise with yarn in front on WS rows

---

SLIP STITCH PATTERN 30

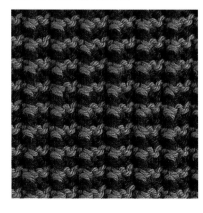

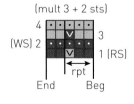

(mult 3 + 2 sts)

To begin: CO with A and knit 1 row.

Color Key

■ = A

■ = B

Stitch Key

□ = K on RS; p on WS

• = K on WS

∨ = Slip st purlwise with yarn in back on RS rows

SLIP STITCH PATTERN 31

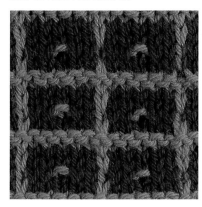

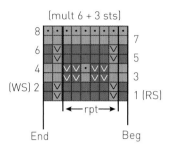

(mult 6 + 3 sts)

End   Beg

To begin: CO with B and knit 1 row.

Color Key

■ = A

■ = B

Stitch Key

□ = K on RS; p on WS

• = P on RS; k on WS

∨ = Slip st purlwise with yarn in back on RS rows; slip st purlwise with yarn in front on WS rows

---

SLIP STITCH PATTERN 32

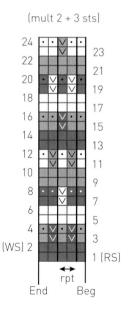

(mult 2 + 3 sts)

End   Beg

To begin: CO with C and knit 1 row.

Color Key

■ = A

■ = B

□ = C

Stitch Key

□ = K on RS; p on WS

• = P on RS; k on WS

∨ = Slip st purlwise with yarn in back on RS rows; slip st purlwise with yarn in front on WS rows

SLIP STITCH PATTERN 33

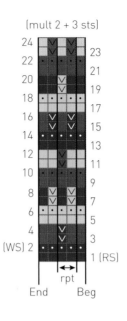

(mult 2 + 3 sts)

To begin: CO with C and purl 1 row.

Color Key

■ = A

■ = B

☐ = C

Stitch Key

☐ = K on RS; p on WS

• = P on RS; k on WS

∨ = Slip st purlwise with yarn in back on RS rows; slip st purlwise with yarn in front on WS rows

SLIP STITCH PATTERN 34

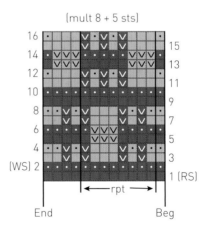

(mult 8 + 5 sts)

To begin: CO with A and purl 1 row.

Color Key

■ = A

■ = B

Stitch Key

☐ = K on RS; p on WS

• = P on RS; k on WS

∨ = Slip st purlwise with yarn in back on RS rows; slip st purlwise with yarn in front on WS rows

SLIP STITCH PATTERN 35

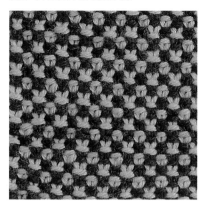

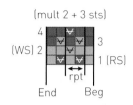

(mult 2 + 3 sts)

End   Beg

To begin: CO with A and purl 1 row.

Color Key

■ = A

■ = B

Stitch Key

□ = K on RS; p on WS

⅄ = Slip st purlwise with yarn in front on RS rows; slip st purlwise with yarn in back on WS rows

SLIP STITCH PATTERN 36

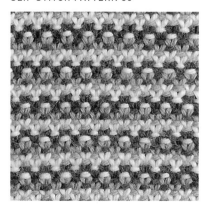

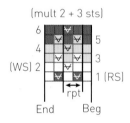

(mult 2 + 3 sts)

End   Beg

To begin: CO with A and purl 1 row.

Color Key

■ = A

■ = B

□ = C

Stitch Key

□ = K on RS; p on WS

⅄ = Slip st purlwise with yarn in front on RS rows; slip st purlwise with yarn in back on WS rows

SLIP STITCH PATTERN 37

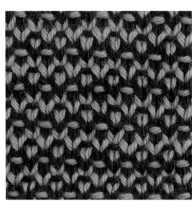

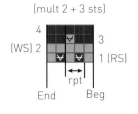

(mult 2 + 3 sts)

End — Beg

rpt

To begin: CO with B and purl 1 row.

Color Key

■ = A

■ = B

Stitch Key

□ = K on RS; p on WS

ᴠ = Slip st purlwise with yarn in front on RS rows; slip st purlwise with yarn in back on WS rows

SLIP STITCH PATTERN 38

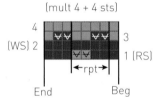

(mult 4 + 4 sts)

End — Beg

rpt

To begin: CO with A and purl 1 row.

Color Key

■ = A

■ = B

Stitch Key

□ = K on RS; p on WS

ᴠ = Slip st purlwise with yarn in front on RS rows

SLIP STITCH PATTERN 39

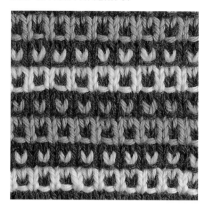

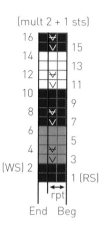

(mult 2 + 1 sts)

To begin: CO with A and purl 1 row.

Color Key

- ■ = A
- ■ = B
- □ = C

Stitch Key

- □ = K on RS; p on WS

- V = Slip st purlwise with
  yarn in back on RS rows

- ⋎ = Slip st purlwise with
  yarn in back on WS rows

SLIP STITCH PATTERN 40

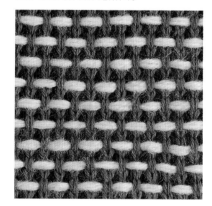

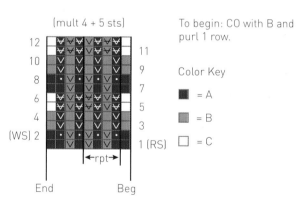

(mult 4 + 5 sts)

To begin: CO with B and
purl 1 row.

Color Key

- ■ = A
- ■ = B
- □ = C

Stitch Key

- □ = K on RS; p on WS

- · = P on RS; k on WS

- V = Slip st purlwise with yarn in back on RS rows; slip st
  purlwise with yarn in front on WS rows

- ⋎ = Slip st purlwise with yarn in front on RS rows; slip st
  purlwise with yarn in back on WS rows

NOTE: *To give a woven effect, in Rows 5, 6, 11,
and 12, Color C is used; the first and last sts
of these rows are worked, but all other sts in
the rows are slipped, either with the yarn in
front or in back.*

STRIPE PATTERN 41

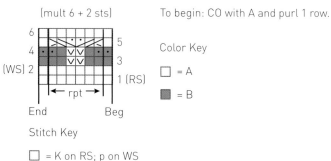

(mult 6 + 2 sts)

To begin: CO with A and purl 1 row.

Color Key

☐ = A

■ = B

Stitch Key

☐ = K on RS; p on WS

• = P on RS; k on WS

∨ = Slip st purlwise with yarn in back on RS rows;
slip st purlwise with yarn in front on WS rows

⟋⟋ = Slip next st onto cn and hold in back; k2; p1 from cn

⟍⟍ = Slip 2 sts onto cn and hold in front; p1; k2 from cn

SLIP STITCH PATTERN 42

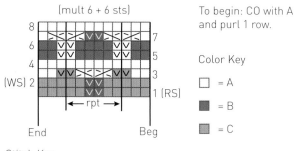

(mult 6 + 6 sts)

To begin: CO with A and purl 1 row.

Color Key

☐ = A

■ = B

■ = C

Stitch Key

☐ = K on RS; P on WS

∨ = Slip st purlwise with yarn in back on RS rows; slip st purlwise
with yarn in front on WS rows

⟩⟨ = Right Twist = Slip next st onto cn and hold in back; k1; k1 from
cn **OR** k2tog, leaving them on LH needle; insert point of RH
needle between these 2 sts and k the first one again

⟩⟨ = Left Twist = Slip next st onto cn and hold in front; k1; k1 from
cn **OR** skip first st and k next st *in back loop*; then k the
skipped st; slip both sts off LH needle tog

SLIP STITCH PATTERN 43

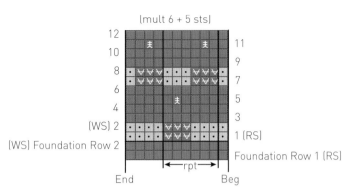

(mult 6 + 5 sts)

To begin: CO with A and purl 1 row.

Color Key

■ = A

■ = B

Stitch Key

□ = K on RS; p on WS

• = P on RS; k on WS

⌄ = Slip st purlwise with yarn in front on RS rows; slip st purlwise with yarn in back on WS rows

⚹ = Insert RH needle under the 2 loose strands several rows below, and knit next st, catching strands

- -

SLIP STITCH PATTERN 44

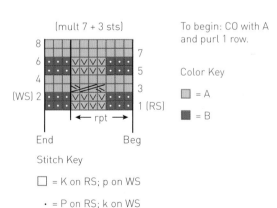

(mult 7 + 3 sts)

To begin: CO with A and purl 1 row.

Color Key

■ = A

■ = B

Stitch Key

□ = K on RS; p on WS

• = P on RS; k on WS

V = Slip st purlwise with yarn in back on RS rows; slip st purlwise with yarn in front on WS rows

⤬ = Slip 2 sts onto cn and hold in back; k2; k2 from cn

SLIP STITCH PATTERN 45

(mult 12 + 7 sts)

To begin: CO with B and knit 1 row.

Color Key

⬜ = A

⬛ = B

Stitch Key

☐ = K on RS; p on WS

· = K on WS

∨ = Slip st purlwise with yarn in back on RS rows; slip st purlwise with yarn in front on WS rows

⟋⟍ = Slip next st onto cn and hold in back; k2; p1 from cn

⟍⟋ = Slip 2 sts onto cn and hold in front; p1; k2 from cn

⟍⟍⟋⟋ = Slip 2 sts onto cn #1 and hold in front; slip next st onto cn #2 and hold in back; k2; slip st from cn #2 onto RH needle with yarn in back; k2 from cn #1

SLIP STITCH PATTERN 46

(mult 4 + 5 sts)

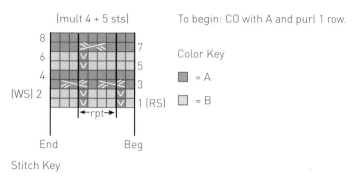

To begin: CO with A and purl 1 row.

Color Key

■ = A

□ = B

Stitch Key

□ = K on RS; p on WS

∨ = Slip st purlwise with yarn in back on RS rows;
slip st purlwise with yarn in front on WS rows

⤬ = Slip 2 sts onto cn and hold in back; k1; k2 from cn

⤬ = Slip next st onto cn and hold in front; k2; k1 from cn

SLIP STITCH PATTERN 47

(mult 6 + 7 sts)

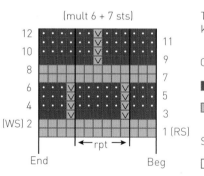

To begin: CO with A and knit 1 row.

Color Key

■ = A

■ = B

Stitch Key

□ = K on RS; p on WS

· = P on RS; k on WS

∨ = Slip st purlwise with yarn in back on RS rows; slip st purlwise with yarn in front on WS rows

SKILL LEVEL
Easy

SIZE
One size

FINISHED MEASUREMENTS
Approximately 12"x 6"/[30.5cm x 15cm]

MATERIALS
Cascade Yarns' *Pastaza:* 4-medium/ worsted weight; 50% wool/50% llama; each approximately 3½ oz/100g and 132 yd/121m). 2 hanks of Concord Grape Handpaint #9930 (A) and 1 hank of Teal #040 (B); (4)

Size 8 (5mm) knitting needles

Size 9 (5.5mm) knitting needles, or size needed to obtain gauge

One pair of 12"/[30.5cm] purse rod handles (Judi & Co's style #LU5 was used on sample clutch)

Matching cotton fabric for lining, ½ yd/[0.5m] (optional)

Pellon *Fusible Fleece* (available at fabric stores), ½ yd/[0.5m] (optional)

Blunt-end yarn needle

GAUGE
18 stitches and 32 rows = 4"/[10cm] in the Mosaic Pattern with larger needles.

To save time, take time to check gauge.

STITCH PATTERNS
Mosaic Pattern (multiple of 10 stitches + 2)
See chart (page 122).

*Stockinette Stitch
(any number of stitches)*
Row 1 (RS): Knit across.

Row 2: Purl across.

Repeat Rows 1 and 2 for the pattern.

Everyday Clutch

Making Mosaic Patterns

Knit up this cool little bag in no time at all! A simple geometric mosaic pattern uses a multicolor yarn to create exquisite texture with only one yarn per row.

NOTE
- When working the Mosaic Pattern, always slip stitches purlwise (page 152).

SUGGESTED ALTERNATE COLORWAYS
Alternate Colorway 1, left: Cascade Yarns' *Pastaza* in Hot Pink #1017 (A) and Raisin #018 (B)

Alternate Colorway 2, right: Heathered Aqua #085 (A) and Lava #046 (B); (4)

 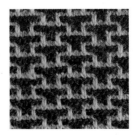

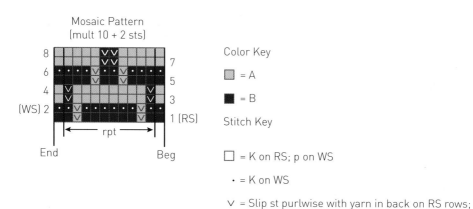

Mosaic Pattern
(mult 10 + 2 sts)

Color Key

☐ = A

■ = B

Stitch Key

☐ = K on RS; p on WS

· = K on WS

∨ = Slip st purlwise with yarn in back on RS rows;
slip st purlwise with yarn in front on WS rows

Back

With the larger needles and A, cast on 52 stitches.

Change to B; work even in the Mosaic Pattern until the piece measures approximately 6"/ [15cm], ending after Row 8 of the pattern.

Change to the smaller needles and B; knit 2 rows.

Next row (RS): Change to A; knit and decrease 5 stitches evenly across the row—47 stitches remain.

Work even in Stockinette Stitch for 13 rows.

Bind off.

Front

Work the same as for the Back.

Gusset

With A, cast on 12 stitches.

Change to B; work even in the Mosaic Pattern until the piece measures approximately 20½"/ [52cm], ending after Row 8 of the pattern.

Bind off.

Finishing

Weave in all remaining yarn tails.

Block the pieces to the finished measurements.

Fold the Stockinette Stitch section over one handle and sew to the wrong side, enclosing the handle.

Repeat for the second handle.

Beginning approximately 1½"/[3.8cm] from the lower edge of the purse rod handles, pin the Gusset to the side edges of the Front and the Back.

With the right sides facing and using the invisible seaming method (page 155), sew the Front and the Back to the Gusset.

Use your fingers to pinch the sides of the Gusset together at the side of the bag to create an inverted pinch pleat on the inside of the bag. Sew into place. Repeat for the other side.

Optional: Cut the lining material and the fusible fleece to fit the bag (approximately 15½" x 15"/ [39.5cm x 38cm]). Iron the fleece to the wrong side of the fabric lining.

Place the lining into the bag and pin it into place, turning ½"/[13mm] to the wrong side along the top edge. Sew the lining into place.

SKILL LEVEL
Intermediate

SIZES
Man's XS (S, M, L, 1X, 2X). Instructions are for the smallest size, with changes for the other sizes noted in parentheses as necessary.

FINISHED MEASUREMENTS
Chest: 39 (43, 48, 52, 56, 61)"/[99 (109, 122, 132, 142, 155)cm]

Length: 26 (27, 27, 27½, 27½, 27½)"/[66 (68.5, 68.5, 70, 70, 70)cm]

MATERIALS
Aurora Yarns/Ornaghi Filati's *Lana D'Irland*: 4-medium/worsted weight; 100% merino wool superwash; each approximately 3½ oz/[100g] and 210 yd/ [192m]. 3 (4, 4, 5, 6, 6) balls of Loden #228 (A), 3 (3, 4, 4, 5, 5) balls of Dark Taupe Heather #732 (B), and 3 (4, 4, 5, 5, 6) balls of Light Taupe Heather #731 (C); (**4**)

Size 6 (4mm) knitting needles

Size 8 (5mm) knitting needles, or size needed to obtain gauge

One 9"/[23cm] zipper

One safety pin

Blunt-end yarn needle

GAUGE
22 stitches and 32 rows = 4"/[10cm] in the Tweed Pattern with larger needles.

To save time, take time to check gauge.

STITCH PATTERNS
Rib Pattern (multiple of 4 stitches + 2)
Row 1 (RS): K2, *p2, k2; repeat from * across.

Row 2: P2, *k2, p2; repeat from * across.

Repeat Rows 1 and 2 for the pattern.

Tweed Pattern (multiple of 4 stitches + 3)
See chart (page 126).

Tweed Boyfriend Sweater

Stranding Yarn to the Front

A simple slip stitch pattern adds just a bit of colorful texture to make this project the perfect knit for your man. It's got enough going on to keep you satisfied as a knitter while creating a sweater he'll still be willing to wear!

NOTES

- When working the Tweed Pattern, always slip stitches purlwise.

- To increase stitches, use the M1-R and M1-L technique (page 151).

- For sweater assembly, refer to the illustration for square-indented sleeve construction on page 156.

SUGGESTED ALTERNATE COLORWAYS
Alternate Colorway 1, left: Aurora Yarns/Ornaghi Filati's *Lana D'Irlanda* in Dusk #753 (A), Cadet Blue #989 (B), and Off-White #028 (C)

Alternate Colorway 2, right: Burgundy #452 (A), Dark Taupe #163 (B), and Camel #171 (C); (**4**)

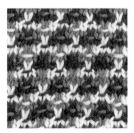 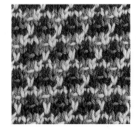

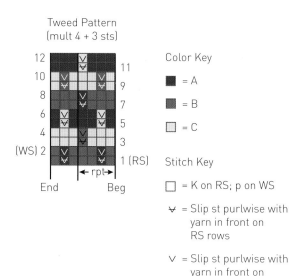

Tweed Pattern
(mult 4 + 3 sts)

Color Key

■ = A

■ = B

□ = C

Stitch Key

□ = K on RS; p on WS

⋎ = Slip st purlwise with
yarn in front on
RS rows

∨ = Slip st purlwise with
yarn in front on
WS rows

Back

With the smaller needles and A, cast on 106 (118, 130, 142, 154, 166) stitches.

Work even in the Rib Pattern until the piece measures approximately 3"/[7.5cm], ending after a wrong-side row.

Change to the larger needles and B; begin working the Tweed Pattern, and increase 1 stitch at the beginning of the 1st row—107 (119, 131, 143, 155, 167) stitches.

Work even until the piece measures approximately 15½"/[39.5cm] from the beginning, ending after a wrong-side row.

SHAPE ARMHOLES

Bind off 12 (12, 16, 16, 20, 24) stitches at the beginning of the next 2 rows—83 (95, 99, 111, 115, 119) stitches remain.

Work even until the armholes measure approximately 9½ (10, 10, 10½, 10½, 10½)"/[24 (25.5, 25.5, 26.5, 26.5, 26.5)cm], ending after a wrong-side row.

SHAPE SHOULDERS

Bind off 5 (7, 7, 9, 9, 10) stitches at the beginning of the next 4 rows, then bind off 5 (6, 7, 8, 9, 9) stitches at the beginning of the next 4 rows—43 stitches remain.

Bind off.

Front

Work the same as for the Back until the armholes measure 2 (2½, 2½, 3, 3, 3)"/[5 (6.5, 6.5, 7.5, 7.5, 7.5)cm], ending after a wrong-side row.

DIVIDE FOR ZIPPER OPENING

Next Row (RS): Work 41 (47, 49, 55, 57, 59) stitches, slip the middle stitch onto the safety pin, join a 2nd ball of yarn and work to the end of the row.

Work both sides at once with separate balls of yarn until the armholes measure approximately 7½ (8, 8, 8½, 8½, 8½)"/[19 (20.5, 20.5, 21.5, 21.5, 21.5)cm], ending after a wrong-side row.

SHAPE NECK

Bind off 9 stitches at each neck edge once; bind off 4 stitches at each neck edge once; bind off 2 stitches at each neck edge twice—24 (30, 32, 38, 40, 42) stitches remain on each side.

Decrease 1 stitch at each neck edge every row 4 times—20 (26, 28, 34, 36, 38) stitches remain on each side.

Work even until the armholes measure the same as for the Back to the shoulders, ending after a wrong-side row.

SHAPE SHOULDERS

Work the same as for the Back.

Sleeves (Make 2)

With the smaller needles and A, cast on 54 stitches.

Work even in the Rib Pattern until the piece measures approximately 2"/[5cm], ending after a wrong-side row.

Change to the larger needles and B; begin working the Tweed Pattern, and increase 1 stitch at the beginning of the 1st row—55 stitches.

Continuing in the established pattern, increase 1 stitch at each side every 4 rows 1 (12, 16, 22, 25, 30) time(s), then every 6 rows 24 (16, 12, 8, 5, 0) times as follows: k1, M1-R, work to last stitch, M1-L, k1, working the new stitches into the Tweed Pattern as they accumulate—105 (111, 111, 115, 115, 115) stitches.

Work even until the Sleeve measures approximately 22½ (22, 22, 22, 22, 21½)"/[57 (56, 56, 56, 56, 54.5)cm].

Bind off.

Finishing

Weave in all remaining yarn tails.

Block all pieces to the finished measurements.

Sew the shoulder seams.

NECKBAND

With the right side facing, using the smaller needles and A, and beginning at the right neck edge at the top of the zipper opening, pick up and knit 110 stitches around the neckline to left neck edge at the top of the zipper opening.

Beginning with Row 2, work even in the Rib Pattern until the neckband measures approximately 3½"/[9cm].

Bind off *loosely* in pattern.

ZIPPER FACING

With the right side facing, using the smaller needles and A, pick up and knit 59 stitches along the left side of the zipper opening, knit the stitch from the safety pin, pick up and knit 59 stitches along the right side of the zipper opening—119 stitches.

Next Row: Bind off knitwise.

Sew in the zipper.

Set in the Sleeves.

Sew the sleeve and side seams.

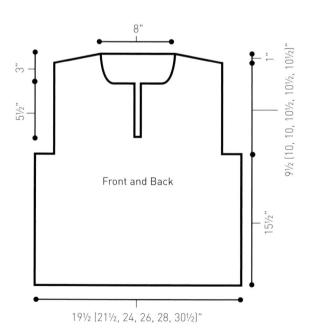

8"

3"

5½"

1"

9½ (10, 10, 10½, 10½, 10½)"

Front and Back

15½"

19½ (21½, 24, 26, 28, 30½)"

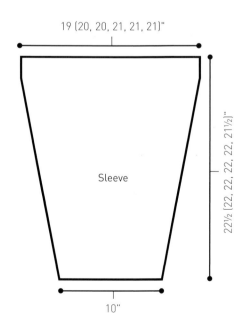

19 (20, 20, 21, 21, 21)"

22½ (22, 22, 22, 22, 21½)"

Sleeve

10"

April's Sweater Dress

Using a Slip Stitch Pattern for Design Emphasis

Knit this cute dress for a special little girl in your life. Its empire waist, wavy edges, and button-up shoulders are sure to make it a favorite!

NOTES

- When working the Textured Slip Stitch Pattern, always slip stitches purlwise.

- To decrease stitches, on right-side rows, use ssk at the beginning of rows and k2tog at the end of rows; on wrong-side rows, use p2tog at the beginning of rows and ssp at the end of rows.

- To increase stitches, use the M1-R and M1-L technique (page 151).

- For sweater assembly, refer to the illustration for set-in sleeve construction on page 156.

SKILL LEVEL
Intermediate

SIZES
Girl's 2 (4, 6). Instructions are for the smallest size, with changes for the other sizes noted in parentheses as necessary.

FINISHED MEASUREMENTS
Chest: 22 (24, 26)"/(56 (61, 66)cm]

Length: 19 (20, 21)"/(48.5 (51, 53.5)cm]

MATERIALS
GGH/Muench Yarns' *Bali:* 3-light/DK weight; 50% cotton/50% acrylic; each approximately 1¾ oz/[50g] and 159 yd/ [145m]. 1 ball of Lemon #107 (A), 5 (5, 6) balls of Tangerine #76 (B), and 1 ball of Lime #78 (C); (3)

Size 4 (3.5mm) knitting needles

Size 5 (3.75mm) knitting needles, or size needed to obtain gauge

Four buttons, 3/8"/[9.5mm] in diameter (JHB International's *Bahia* #15235 was used on sample garment)

Two stitch holders

Blunt-end yarn needle

(continued on next page.)

GAUGE

22 stitches and 30 rows = 4"/[10cm] in Stockinette Stitch with the larger needles.

24 stitches and 36 rows = 4"/[10cm] in Textured Slip Stitch Pattern with the larger needles.

To save time, take time to check gauge.

STITCH PATTERNS

Border Pattern (multiple of 7 stitches + 1)
Row 1 (RS): K1, *yo, k1, ssk, k2tog, k1, yo, k1; repeat from * across.

Row 2: Knit across.

Repeat Rows 1 and 2 for the pattern.

*Stockinette Stitch
(any number of stitches)*
Row 1 (RS): Knit across.

Row 2: Purl across.

Repeat Rows 1 and 2 for the pattern.

Garter Stitch (any number of stitches)
Pattern Row: Knit across.

*Textured Slip Stitch Pattern
(multiple of 6 stitches + 5)*
See chart (page 131).

SUGGESTED ALTERNATE COLORWAYS

Alternate Colorway 1, left: GGH/Muench Yarns' *Bali* in Fuchsia #87 (A), Light Pink #68 (B), and White #3 (C)

Alternate Colorway 2, right: Misty Blue #98 (A), Turquoise #101 (B), and Delft Blue #58 (C); **3**

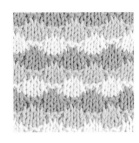 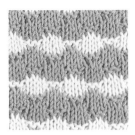

Back

With the smaller needles and A, cast on 85 (92, 99) stitches.

Work the Border Pattern for 6 rows.

Change to the larger needles and B; work even in Stockinette Stitch until the piece measures approximately 12½ (13½, 14½)"/[32 (34.5, 37)cm], ending after a wrong-side row.

Next Row (RS): Change to the smaller needles and knit across, decreasing 30 (32, 34) stitches evenly across the row—55 (60, 65) stitches remain.

Continue in Garter Stitch until the piece measures approximately 13½ (14½, 15½)"/[34.5 (37, 39.5)cm] from the beginning, ending after a wrong-side row.

Next Row (RS): Change to the larger needles and A; work Row 1 of the Textured Slip Stitch pattern, increasing 10 (11, 12) stitches evenly across the row—65 (71, 77) stitches.

Work even in the Textured Slip Stitch Pattern until the piece measures approximately 14½ (15, 15½)"/[37 (38, 39.5)cm] from the beginning, ending after a wrong-side row.

SHAPE ARMHOLES

Bind off 3 stitches at the beginning of the next 2 rows; bind off 2 stitches at the beginning of the next 2 rows—55 (61, 67) stitches remain.

Decrease 1 stitch at each side of every row 4 times—47 (53, 59) stitches remain.

Work even until the armholes measure approximately 4 (4½, 5)"/[10 (11.5, 12.5)cm], ending after a wrong-side row.

SHAPE NECK

Next Row (RS): Work 9 (12, 15) stitches, join a 2nd ball of yarn and bind off the middle 29 stitches, work to the end of the row.

Next Row (WS): Working both sides at once with separate balls of yarn, decrease 1 stitch at each neck edge—8 (11, 14) stitches remain on each side.

Work even until the armholes measure approximately 4½ (5, 5½)"/[11.5 (12.5, 14)cm], ending after a wrong-side row.

Next Row (RS): Bind off 8 (11, 14) stitches for the right shoulder; slip the remaining 8 (11, 14) stitches onto a holder for the left shoulder.

Front

Work the same as for the Back until the armholes measure approximately 1½ (2, 2½)"/[4 (5, 6.5)cm], ending after a wrong-side row.

SHAPE NECK

Next Row (RS): Work 16 (19, 22) stitches, join a 2nd ball of yarn and bind off the middle 15 stitches, work to the end of the row.

Working both sides at once with separate balls of yarn, bind off 3 stitches at each neck edge once, then bind off 2 stitches at each neck edge once—11 (14, 17) stitches remain.

Decrease 1 stitch at each neck edge every row 3 times—8 (11, 14) stitches remain on each side.

Textured Slip Stitch Pattern
(mult 6 + 5 sts)

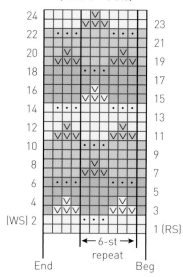

← 6-st →
repeat

End   Beg

Color Key

☐ = A

▨ = B

▨ = C

Stitch Key

☐ = K on RS; p on WS

• = K on WS

∨ = Slip st purlwise with yarn in back on RS rows; slip st purlwise with yarn in front on WS rows

Work even until the armholes measure approximately 4½ (5, 5½)"/[11.5 (12.5, 14)cm], ending after a wrong-side row.

Slip the remaining 8 (11, 14) stitches onto a holder for the left shoulder.

Work even on the right shoulder stitches until the armhole measures approximately 5½ (6, 6½)"/[14 (15, 16.5)cm], ending after a wrong-side row.

Bind off.

Sleeves (Make 2)

With the smaller needles and A, cast on 57 stitches.

Work the Border Pattern for 6 rows.

Change to the larger needles and B; begin working the Textured Slip Stitch Pattern on Row 9, and increase 1 stitch at each side of every row 1 (1, 3) time(s), then every other row 1 (1, 0) time as follows: K1, M1-R, work in pattern to the last stitch, M1-L, k1, working all new stitches into the Textured Slip Stitch Pattern as they accumulate—61 (61, 63) stitches.

Work even until the piece measures approximately 1½ (1½, 2)"/[4 (4, 5)cm], ending after a wrong-side row.

SHAPE CAP

Bind off 3 stitches at the beginning of the next 2 rows—55 (55, 57) stitches remain.

Decrease 1 stitch at each side of every other row 12 (12, 11) times, then every row 5 (5, 7) times—21 stitches remain.

Bind off 3 stitches at the beginning of the next 4 rows—9 stitches remain.

Bind off.

Finishing

Weave in all remaining yarn tails.

Block all pieces to the finished measurements.

Sew the right shoulder seam.

NECKBAND

With the right side facing, using the smaller needles and A, pick up and knit 75 stitches along the neckline.

Work even in Garter Stitch until the neckband measures approximately 1"/[2.5cm].

Bind off.

BUTTON BAND

With the right side facing, using the smaller needles and A, pick up and knit 5 stitches along the edge of the neckband, then knit the 8 (10, 14) stitches from the back left shoulder holder—13 (15, 19) stitches total.

Work even in Garter Stitch until the button band measures approximately 1"/[2.5cm].

Bind off.

Place markers for 4 evenly spaced buttons along the button band.

BUTTONHOLE BAND

Work the same as for the button band until the buttonhole band measures ½"/[13mm].

Make 4 buttonholes opposite the button markers by working (k2tog, yo).

Complete the same as for the button band.

Overlap the buttonhole with the button band and sew the armhole ends together.

Set in the Sleeves.

Sew the sleeve and side seams.

Sew on the buttons.

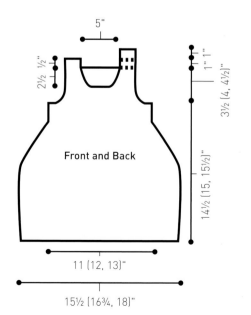

Front and Back

5"

2½ ½"

1" 1"

3½ (4, 4½)"

14½ (15, 15½)"

11 (12, 13)"

15½ (16¾, 18)"

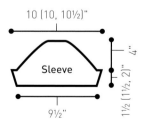

Sleeve

10 (10, 10½)"

4"

1½ (1½, 2)"

9½"

SKILL LEVEL
Easy

SIZE
One size

FINISHED MEASUREMENTS
Circumference: 10½"/[26.5cm]

Length: 12"/[30.5cm]

MATERIALS
Brown Sheep Company's *Lambs Pride Superwash Worsted*: 4-medium/worsted weight; 100% superwash wool; each approximately 3½ oz/[100g] and 200 yd/[183m]. 1 ball *each* of Fuchsia Blaze #177 (A) and Corn Silk #13 (B); (**4**)

Size 8 (5 mm) knitting needles, or size needed to obtain gauge

Ribbon for tie, ½"/[13mm] wide

Blunt-end yarn needle

GAUGE
18 stitches and 40 rounds = 4"/[10cm] in Mosaic Pattern.

To save time, take time to check gauge.

STITCH PATTERNS
Border Pattern (multiple of 6 stitches + 2)
See chart (page 135).

Mosaic Pattern (multiple of 4 stitches + 2)
See chart (page 135).

*Stockinette Stitch
(any number of stitches)*
Row 1 (RS): Knit across.

Row 2: Purl across.

Repeat Rows 1 and 2 for the pattern.

Op Art Wine Cozy

Practicing Basic Slip Stitch Techniques

Wrap your favorite bottle of wine in this pretty cozy. It provides the perfect presentation for a hostess gift.

NOTE

• For quick and easy finishing, rather than cutting the yarns after each stripe, carry them loosely up the wrong side.

SUGGESTED ALTERNATE COLORWAYS

Alternate Colorway 1, left: Brown Sheep Company's *Lambs Pride Superwash Worsted* in Serendipity Turquoise #36 (A) and Red Baron #81 (B)

Alternate Colorway 2, right: Blueberry Sorbet #130 (A) and Blue Heaven #92 (B); (4)

Wine Cozy

With A, cast on 50 stitches.

Begin the Border Pattern and work even until the piece measures approximately 3"/[7.5cm].

Change to B, begin the Mosaic Pattern, and continue even until the piece measures approximately 12"/[30.5cm] from the beginning, ending after Row 10 of the pattern.

Change to A, and work 5 rows in Stockinette Stitch.

CREATE RIDGE

Next Row (WS): *Use the left-hand needle to pick up the purl bump of the next stitch 6 rows down, and purl this stitch together with the next stitch on the needle; repeat from * around.

DECREASE FOR BASE

Next Row (RS): K1, *k2tog, k3, ssk; repeat from *—36 stitches remain.

Next Row: Purl across.

Next Row: K1, *k2tog, k1, ssk; repeat from *—22 stitches remain.

Next Row: Purl across.

Next Row: K1, *ssk, k1; repeat from *—15 stitches remain.

Next Row: Purl across.

Next Row: K1, *ssk; repeat from *—8 stitches remain.

Next Row: *P2tog; repeat from *—4 stitches remain.

Cut the yarn, leaving an 18"/[45.5cm] tail for sewing. Draw the yarn through the remaining 4 stitches on the needle and pull tight.

Finishing

Weave in all remaining yarn tails.

Sew the seam.

Thread the ribbon through the bottom row of eyelet holes. Trim the ribbon to the desired length.

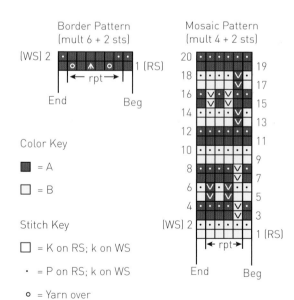

Border Pattern
(mult 6 + 2 sts)

(WS) 2   1 (RS)
← rpt →
End   Beg

Mosaic Pattern
(mult 4 + 2 sts)

Color Key

▮ = A

☐ = B

Stitch Key

☐ = K on RS; k on WS

· = P on RS; k on WS

o = Yarn over

⋀ = Slip 2 sts at once knitwise, k1, p2sso

∨ = Slip st purlwise with yarn in back on RS rows; slip st purlwise with yarn in front on WS rows

SKILL LEVEL
Intermediate

SIZES
S (M, L, 1X, 2X). Instructions are for
the smallest size, with changes for the
other sizes noted in parentheses
as necessary.

FINISHED MEASUREMENTS
Bust (buttoned): 36 (39, 42½, 46, 50)"/[91
(99, 108, 117, 127)cm]

Length: 18 (18½, 19, 19½, 19½)"/[45.5
(47, 48.5, 49.5, 49.5)cm]

MATERIALS
Aurora Yarns/Ornaghi Filati's *Land:
5*-bulky weight; 50% wool/10%
alpaca/40% acrylic; each approximately
1¾ oz/[50g] and 66 yd/[60m]. 6 (8, 9, 10,
11) balls of Burgundy #123 (A); 3 (4, 4, 5,
5) balls of Medium Rose #120 (B); 2 (3,
3, 4, 4) balls of Light Rose #104 (C);
1 (2, 2, 3, 3) balls of Cream #100 (D); (⑤)

Size 11 (8mm) knitting needles, or size
needed to obtain gauge

Size 11 (8mm) 24"/[60cm] circular
knitting needle, or size needed
to obtain gauge

Stitch markers

Blunt-end yarn needle

Two 1½"/[4cm] buttons (Aurora Yarns'
style #FB159E was used
on sample garment)

GAUGE
13 stitches and 24 rows = 4"/[10cm]
in the Mosaic Pattern.

To save time, take time to check gauge.

STITCH PATTERNS
Mosaic Pattern
See charts (page 139–141).

Garter Stitch
Pattern Row: Knit across.

Cleo's Jacket

Colorblocking to Flatter Your Figure

You'll whip up this little jacket in no time at all, since
thick yarn and big needles mean quick knitting. Clever
placement of darker contrast colors toward the bottom
of this garment makes it especially flattering.

NOTES

- The instructions include one selvage stitch at each
  side. These stitches are worked in Garter Stitch in the
  same color used to work the pattern across the row and
  are not reflected in the final measurements. Work all
  decreases inside these selvage stitches.

- To increase stitches, use M1 technique (page 151).

- For the colorwork, use the slip stitch technique throughout.

- After Row 100 of the Mosaic Pattern chart has been
  completed, repeat from Row 80, if necessary, until the
  piece measures the required length.

- For the sweater assembly, refer to the illustration for
  set-in sleeve construction on page 156.

Back

With A, cast on 61 (65, 71, 77, 83) stitches.

Working the first and last stitches in Garter Stitch, then beginning and ending where indicated on the chart for your size, work even in the Mosaic Pattern until the piece measures approximately 10"/[25.5cm], ending after a wrong-side row. *Make a note of which row you ended on.*

SHAPE ARMHOLES

Continuing the pattern as established, bind off 4 (5, 6, 7, 7) stitches at the beginning of the next 2 rows; bind off 2 (2, 3, 3, 4) stitches at the beginning of the next 2 rows—49 (51, 53, 57, 61) stitches remain.

Decrease 1 stitch at each side of every row 1 (1, 1, 3, 3) time(s), then every other row 3 (3, 4, 3, 4) times—41 (43, 43, 45, 47) stitches remain.

Work even until the armholes measure approximately 7 (7½, 8, 8½, 8½)"/[18 (19, 20.5, 21.5, 21.5) cm], ending after a wrong-side row.

SHAPE SHOULDERS

Bind off 3 (4, 4, 4, 4) stitches at the beginning of the next 4 rows, then bind off 4 (3, 3, 4, 5) stitches at the beginning of the next 2 rows—21 stitches remain.

Bind off.

Left Front

With A, cast on 35 (37, 39, 43, 45) stitches.

Working the first and last stitches in Garter Stitch, then beginning and ending where indicated on the chart for your size, work even in the Mosaic Pattern until the piece measures approximately 10"/[25.5cm], ending after the same row that you ended on for the Back before working the armhole.

SHAPE ARMHOLE

Bind off 4 (5, 6, 7, 7) stitches at the armhole edge once, then bind off 2 (2, 3, 3, 4) stitches at the armhole edge once—29 (30, 30, 33, 34) stitches remain.

Decrease 1 stitch at the armhole edge every row 1 (1, 1, 3, 3) time(s), then every other row 3 (3, 4, 3, 4) times—25 (26, 25, 27, 27) stitches remain.

Work even until the armhole measures approximately 5 (5½, 6, 6½, 6½)"/[12.5 (14, 15, 16.5, 16.5) cm], ending after a right-side row.

SHAPE NECK

Bind off 5 (5, 4, 5, 4) stitches at the neck edge once; bind 4 stitches at the neck edge once; bind off 2 stitches at the neck edge twice, then decrease 1 stitch at the neck edge every row twice—10 (11, 11, 12, 13) stitches remain.

Work even until the armhole measures approximately 7 (7½, 8, 8½, 8½)"/[18 (19, 20.5, 21.5, 21.5) cm], ending after a wrong-side row.

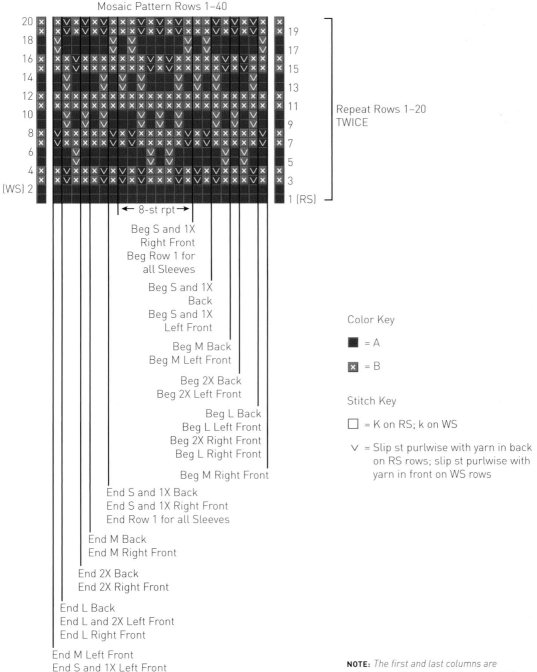

Mosaic Pattern Rows 1–40

Repeat Rows 1–20 TWICE

← 8-st rpt →

Beg S and 1X
Right Front
Beg Row 1 for
all Sleeves

Beg S and 1X
Back
Beg S and 1X
Left Front

Beg M Back
Beg M Left Front

Beg 2X Back
Beg 2X Left Front

Beg L Back
Beg L Left Front
Beg 2X Right Front
Beg L Right Front

Beg M Right Front

End S and 1X Back
End S and 1X Right Front
End Row 1 for all Sleeves

End M Back
End M Right Front

End 2X Back
End 2X Right Front

End L Back
End L and 2X Left Front
End L Right Front

End M Left Front
End S and 1X Left Front

Color Key

■ = A

☒ = B

Stitch Key

□ = K on RS; k on WS

∨ = Slip st purlwise with yarn in back
on RS rows; slip st purlwise with
yarn in front on WS rows

NOTE: *The first and last columns are
selvage sts. Knit these sts every row in the
designated color, then continue with the
pattern, beginning and ending at the point
indicated on the chart.*

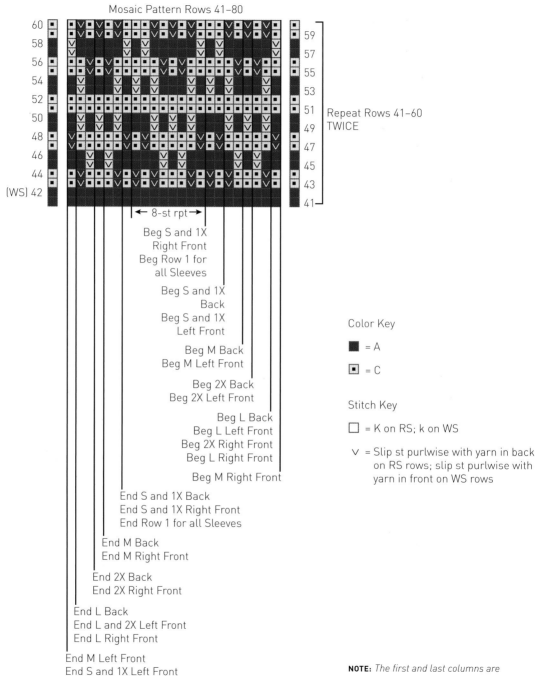

Mosaic Pattern Rows 41–80

Repeat Rows 41–60 TWICE

← 8-st rpt →

Beg S and 1X
Right Front
Beg Row 1 for
all Sleeves

Beg S and 1X
Back
Beg S and 1X
Left Front

Beg M Back
Beg M Left Front

Beg 2X Back
Beg 2X Left Front

Beg L Back
Beg L Left Front
Beg 2X Right Front
Beg L Right Front

Beg M Right Front

End S and 1X Back
End S and 1X Right Front
End Row 1 for all Sleeves

End M Back
End M Right Front

End 2X Back
End 2X Right Front

End L Back
End L and 2X Left Front
End L Right Front

End M Left Front
End S and 1X Left Front

Color Key

■ = A

▣ = C

Stitch Key

□ = K on RS; k on WS

V = Slip st purlwise with yarn in back
on RS rows; slip st purlwise with
yarn in front on WS rows

NOTE: The first and last columns are
selvage sts. Knit these sts every row in the
designated color, then continue with the
pattern, beginning and ending at the point
indicated on the chart.

Mosaic Pattern Rows 81–100

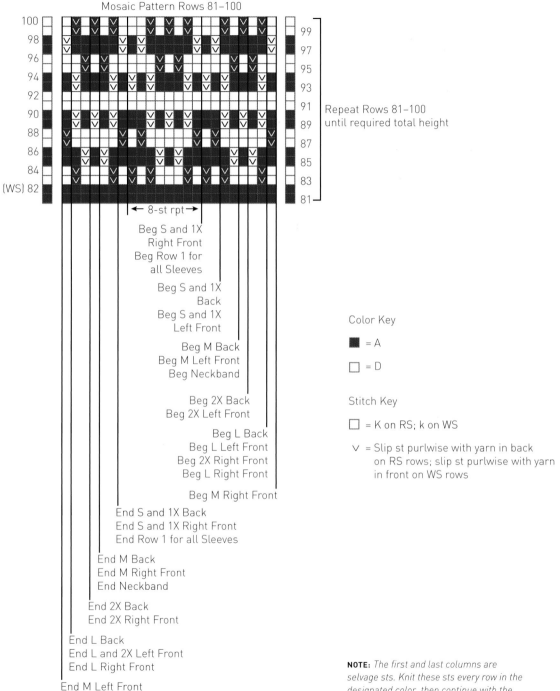

Repeat Rows 81–100
until required total height

← 8-st rpt →

Beg S and 1X
Right Front
Beg Row 1 for
all Sleeves

Beg S and 1X
Back
Beg S and 1X
Left Front

Beg M Back
Beg M Left Front
Beg Neckband

Beg 2X Back
Beg 2X Left Front

Beg L Back
Beg L Left Front
Beg 2X Right Front
Beg L Right Front

Beg M Right Front

End S and 1X Back
End S and 1X Right Front
End Row 1 for all Sleeves

End M Back
End M Right Front
End Neckband

End 2X Back
End 2X Right Front

End L Back
End L and 2X Left Front
End L Right Front

End M Left Front
End S and 1X Left Front

Color Key

■ = A

□ = D

Stitch Key

□ = K on RS; k on WS

∨ = Slip st purlwise with yarn in back
on RS rows; slip st purlwise with yarn
in front on WS rows

NOTE: *The first and last columns are
selvage sts. Knit these sts every row in the
designated color, then continue with the
pattern, beginning and ending at the point
indicated on the chart.*

SHAPE SHOULDER

Bind off 3 (4, 4, 4, 4) stitches at the shoulder edge twice.

Work 1 row even.

Bind off the remaining 4 (3, 3, 4, 5) stitches.

Place a marker ¼"/(6mm) down from the beginning of the front neck shaping.

Right Front

Work the same as for the Left Front *except* reverse all shaping and make 1 buttonhole on a right-side row opposite the marker on the Left Front as follows: Work 2 stitches in pattern, bind off the next 3 stitches, then continue in the pattern as established to the end of the row. On the subsequent row, cast on 3 stitches over the bound-off stitches of the previous row.

Sleeve (Make 2)

With A, cast on 51 stitches.

Working the first and last stitches in Garter Stitch, then beginning and ending where indicated on the chart for the Sleeves, work the Mosaic Pattern over the middle 49 stitches.

For Sizes S, M, and L Only

Continuing in the pattern as established, decrease 1 stitch at each side every 16 (16, 20) rows 3 (3, 2) times—45 (45, 47) stitches remain.

For All Sizes

Work even in the pattern as established on 45 (45, 47, 51, 51) stitches until the piece measures approximately 10"/(25.5cm), ending after the same row that you ended on for the Back before working the armhole.

SHAPE CAP

Bind off 4 (5, 6, 7, 7) stitches at the beginning of the next 2 rows—37 (35, 35, 37, 37) stitches remain.

Decrease 1 stitch at each side every 4 rows 3 (6, 7, 8, 8) times, then every other row 5 (1, 0, 0, 0) time(s)—21 stitches remain.

Bind off 3 stitches at the beginning of the next 4 rows—9 stitches remain.

Bind off.

Finishing

Weave in all remaining yarn tails.

Block all pieces to the finished measurements.

Sew the shoulder seams.

NECKBAND

With the right side facing and A, pick up and knit 55 stitches along the neckline.

Next Row (WS): With A, knit across.

Working the first and last stitches in Garter Stitch, work Row 83 of the Mosaic Pattern, beginning and ending where indicated on the chart for the neckband.

Continue working the pattern through Row 100, *and at the same time,* when the neckband measures approximately 2½"/(6.5cm), ending after a wrong-side row, make 1 buttonhole as follows:

Buttonhole Row (RS): Work the first 2 stitches of the row, bind off the next 3 stitches, work to the end of the row.

Next Row: Work to the bound-off stitches of the previous row, cast on 3 stitches over the bound-off stitches, work the last 2 stitches.

After Row 100 has been completed, work Rows 81 and 82 once more.

Bind off.

Set in the Sleeves.

Sew the sleeve and side seams.

Sew on the buttons.

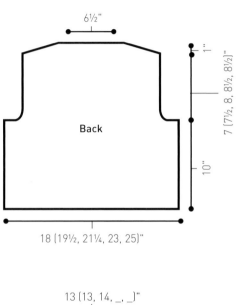

Back

6½"

7 (7½, 8, 8½, 8½)"

10"

18 (19½, 21¼, 23, 25)"

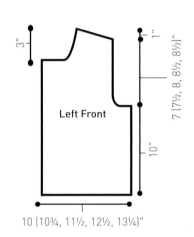

Left Front

3"

1"

7 (7½, 8, 8½, 8½)"

10"

10 (10¾, 11½, 12½, 13¼)"

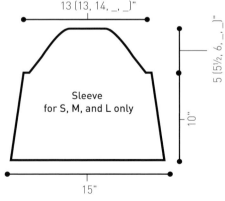

Sleeve
for S, M, and L only

13 (13, 14, _, _)"

5 (5½, 6, _, _)"

10"

15"

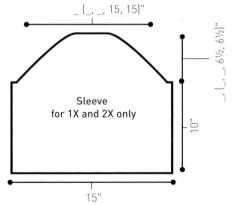

Sleeve
for 1X and 2X only

_ (_, _, 15, 15)"

_ (_, _, 6½, 6½)"

10"

15"

General Techniques

Since everyone knits at a different skill level, this section provides instructions for many of the specific techniques used throughout this book. If a design excites you but some of the techniques used in it seem unfamiliar, please just go for it! Let your knitter's curiosity encourage you to learn new skills and grow. For complete technical information on the different color-knitting techniques, see individual chapters of this book.

Knitting Charts as a Foreign Language: A Crash Course in Translation

A knitting chart is simply a visual representation of knitted fabric. It allows you to see quickly how many stitches are involved in a pattern and to understand what the color pattern will look like as you knit. At first, knitting charts and their symbols might seem like a completely foreign language. Actually, they're simple to translate, and using them will definitely make your knitting easier and faster. Much like reading music, deciphering the charts and their symbols will become natural, and you'll become "fluent" with practice. The charted symbols are easier for the eye to pick up, or "read," than long paragraphs of text. And, of course, since they are visual, they're the perfect way to present color patterns!

A Short Grammar Lesson

Knitting charts are simple grids. Each square of the grid corresponds to one stitch, and each row of squares corresponds to one row of stitches. However, we read these grids from the bottom edge up, a way that often seems backward to first-timers. The first row begins at the bottom of the chart, and the last row ends at the top.

Right-side rows (the rows that face the public side of the fabric) are read from right to left, in the same order that stitches present themselves on the left-hand knitting needle. The following chart shows the order that stitches will be worked for Row 1, a right-side row, in a chart.

Of course, at the end of this first row, you flip your knitting before starting the next row, and the wrong side of the fabric faces you. Physically, the first stitch of this wrong-side row is the last stitch of the right-side row you just completed. Therefore, wrong-side rows on charts are read in the opposite direction, from left to right, as shown below.

When working in the round rather than back and forth in rows, the right side of the fabric always faces you, so all rows of the chart, or all rounds of knitting, are read from right to left.

In some charts, bold vertical lines indicate the stitch repeat; and if extra stitches are required on each side to center the pattern, they are shown to the left and the right of the repeat. For example, to work the sample shown in the following chart, you'd start at the lower right-hand corner, reading from right to left and working the 4-stitch repeat between the two bold lines as many times as necessary to knit across your fabric. Then you would end the row with the stitch represented in this sample chart by the star. This stitch sits outside the stitch repeat and so is worked once per row. It is the *last* stitch of every right-side row; and because wrong-side rows are read from left to right, it is the *first* stitch of these rows.

Color-knitting patterns often employ such repeats within charts. In the Spring into Stripes Pullover (page 62), for example, the Textured

color PLAY

When working from a kintting chart, you may find it helpful to draw arrows on the left-hand side of even-numbered wrong-side rows as a visual reminder that you'll be reading them from left to right. You can even put arrows on the right-hand side of odd-numbered right-side rows, too. Remember, you'll be knitting in what might feel like a foreign language at first. Use any visual clue you can to help you get acquainted with it!

Stripe Pattern requires a 6-stitch repeat *plus* 4 extra stitches on the left side and 1 extra stitch on the right side. These extra stitches are necessary in order to center the pattern properly.

Note: Sometimes, individual pieces or sizes of the same garment will have different beginning and ending places within the stitch pattern. For example, in Cleo's Jacket (page 136), each size begins at a different spot in the chart. But don't worry! Instructions with the chart tell you exactly what to do. When reading a chart, begin and end where indicated for that particular piece of the garment for the size you are knitting.

The Vocabulary List

Each symbol on a chart indicates the way a stitch or group of stitches will be worked, and the arrangement of symbols on the chart determines the stitch pattern. Different colored squares indicate different colors of yarn. If the yarns are rather close in hue, there will be symbols in addition to different colors to help you differentiate between them. Every designer and editor uses a different set of symbols to represent the same knitting maneuvers. Just think about them as unique "dialects" of this foreign language! Fortunately, chart keys neatly decipher all symbols used in charts, from the most common stitches to the most advanced, making even unfamiliar symbols easy to follow.

Designer's Workshop
Hints for Easy Chart Reading

Here are some tips and tricks I've gathered from my workshop participants as I travel the country:

• Enlarge your charts on a photocopier. Stitch symbols will be easier to see and the charts clearer to read.

• Use stitch markers. Some patterns include instructions to place stitch markers on your knitting needles, but you can use markers in any pattern to separate pattern repeats or panels as you knit. They can help you keep track of how many repeats you've completed—and how many you still need to work.

• Use a row counter. When looking from chart to instruction to knitting needles, it's easy to lose your place. Enter the lowly row counter to the rescue! A simple click of the counter when you finish each row means that you'll never lose your place on the chart again. If you have panels across the width of your fabric with different row repeats, use a separate row counter for each one.

The charts for stitch patterns in this book use symbols that visually resemble the way the resulting stitches will appear once knitted. The symbol for a knit stitch, for example, is a blank box, mimicking the flat appearance of the knit stitch itself; the dot symbol for a purl stitch depicts the bumpy appearance of a purled stitch. In slip stitch charts, the stitches of one color that are pulled up to the height of a stripe that's knitted in another color are shown in their *original* color. Just by quickly scanning the chart, you can visualize the knitted fabric.

All rows in charts are shown *as they appear on the public side of the fabric*. Consequently, the same symbol means different things on right-side and wrong-side rows. The blank box, for instance, represents a knit stitch on a right-side row; but if you're on a wrong-side row and want the stitch to appear as a knit stitch on the reverse side of the fabric, you must purl it. If a symbol is used on both right- and wrong-side rows of the chart, the chart key will tell you which knitting maneuver to use where. There's no need to memorize anything!

Sometimes a pattern will specify a "preparation row" (see Dip Stitch Patterns on page 42 and Tuck Stitch Patterns on page 44, for examples). A preparation row is a set-up row that is worked once and is not part of the pattern repeat.

It's worth taking the time to learn, and to practice, knitting from charts. Eventually, you might even find yourself translating long, wordy patterns into symbols before beginning to knit. I'll bet that with some practice—and yes, a little bit of patience—you'll find knitting from charts easy, fast, and maybe even fun!

Comprehensive Glossary of Symbols

☐ = K on RS; p on WS

• = P on RS; k on WS

V = Slip st purlwise with yarn in back on RS rows; slip st purlwise with yarn in front on WS rows

⩹ = Slip st purlwise with yarn in front on RS rows; slip st purlwise with yarn in back on WS rows

O = Yarn over

V = (Increase from 1 st to 2 sts) = Knit into front and then into back of st

⋀ = K2tog on RS; p2tog on WS

⋋ = Ssk on RS; ssp on WS

⋆ = P2tog on RS; k2tog on WS

⋀ = S2kp2 = Central Double Decrease = Slip 2 sts at once knitwise, k1, p2sso

8/ = Elongated Dip St = Insert right-hand needle into st 8 rows below and knit a st, leaving it on right-hand needle; k next st; pass the elongated dip st over the knitted st

6/ = Elongated Dip St = Insert right-hand needle into st 6 rows below and knit a st, leaving it on right-hand needle; k next st; pass the elongated dip st over the knitted st

⋒ = Knit st in the row below

⟨4⟩ = Tuck St = Drop st off LH needle and, using tip of RH needle, unravel 4 rows down; insert RH needle into the live st and knit it, catching the 4 loose strands into the st as you knit

| = Textured Tuck St = Drop st off LH needle and, using tip of RH needle, unravel 4 rows down; insert RH needle into the live st and purl it, catching the 4 loose strands into the st as you purl

✕ = Right Twist = Slip next st onto cn and hold in back; k1; k1 from cn or k2tog, leaving them on LH needle; insert point of RH needle between these 2 sts and k the first one again

✕ = Left Twist = Slip next st onto cn and hold in front; k1; k1 from cn or skip first st and k next st in back loop; then k the skipped st; slip both sts off LH needle together

✕ = Slip 2 sts onto cn and hold in back; k2; k2 from cn

✕ = Slip next st onto cn and hold in back; k2; p1 from cn

✕ = Slip 2 sts onto cn and hold in front; p1; k2 from cn

✕ = Slip 2 sts onto cn #1 and hold in front; slip next st onto cn #2 and hold in back; k2; slip st from cn #2 onto RH needle with yarn in back; k2 from cn #1

✕ = Slip 2 sts onto cn and hold in back; k1; k2 from cn

✕ = Slip next st onto cn and hold in front; k2; k1 from cn

Abbreviations List

Following is a list of abbreviations used in the charts of this book. Many of the techniques are discussed in the Knitting Techniques section (page 150).

cm   centimeter(s)

cn   cable needle

g   gram(s)

k   knit

k2tog   knit the next 2 stitches together; this is a right-slanting decrease

LH   left-hand

mm   millimeter(s)

M1   Make 1 (increase)

M1-L   Make 1 slanting to the left (increase)

M1-R   Make 1 slanting to the right (increase)

mult   multiple

oz   ounce(s)

patt(s)   pattern(s)

p   purl

prep   preparation row

p2tog   purl the next 2 stitches together; this is a right-slanting decrease

rem   remain(ing)

rib   ribbing

RH   right-hand

rnd(s)   round(s)

rpt   repeat

RS   right side (of work)

s2kp2   slip 2 stitches together knitwise, k1, pass the 2 slipped stitches over; this is a centered double decrease

sl   slip stitch from the left-hand needle to the right-hand needle; the convention is to do so purlwise unless otherwise instructed in the pattern

ssk   slip the next 2 stitches knitwise, one at a time from the left-hand needle to the right-hand one, insert the left-hand needle tip into the fronts of both slipped stitches to knit them together from this position; this is a left-slanting decrease

ssp   slip the next 2 stitches knitwise, one at a time from the left-hand needle to the right-hand one, return both stitches to left-hand needle and insert the right-hand needle into them from left to right and from back to front to purl them together through their back loops; this is a left-slanting decrease

st(s)   stitch(es)

tog   together

WS   wrong side (of work)

yd(s)   yard(s)

yo   yarn over

*   repeat instructions after asterisk or between asterisks across row or for as many times as instructed

( )   alternate measurements and/or instructions for different sizes; these parentheses also mean you should repeat instructions within parentheses for as many times as instructed

[ ]   these brackets indicate the separation between empirical and metric measurements in the pattern text

How to Use the Pattern Treasuries

To use a stitch pattern in the Pattern Treasuries on pages 53–61 and pages 95–119, make a swatch that's at least two pattern repeats wide, follow the chart until you've worked through all rows of the chart at least twice, and then measure your gauge. Do not round this number—fractional stitches add up when factored over an entire piece of fabric. If you're using several stitch patterns within a single project, knit and measure a separate gauge swatch for each of them.

When working with some patterns, especially those with slipped or cabled stitches, it can sometimes be difficult to count your stitches. In these instances, simply measure one stitch repeat across; divide the number of stitches involved by that measurement to find the gauge.

For example, to check the gauge of a swatch of Slip Stitch Pattern 47, you would cast on at least 19 stitches. Repeat Rows 1–12 of the chart at least twice, and then bind off. Lay your swatch flat and measure the width from the right-hand edge of one slipped stitch in Rows 9–12 to the right-hand edge of the adjacent one—one complete stitch repeat. If that measurement is, say, 2"/[5cm], then your stitch gauge is 6 stitches divided by 2"/[5cm], or 3 stitches to the inch. If, however, you're using thicker yarn, the width of those same 6 stitches might be 3½"/[9cm], so your stitch gauge would be 6 stitches divided by 3½"/[9cm], or about 1¾ stitches to the inch.

Remember that if you plan to wash and block your project pieces, it's important to take the time to treat your gauge swatch in the same manner before measuring it. Yarn often behaves differently after washing. Some fibers become limp while others bloom; some will contract lengthwise or widthwise. Consider your gauge swatch the perfect opportunity to preview a tiny piece of your completed project.

Once you determine an accurate stitch gauge, just multiply that gauge by the desired width of your fabric to find the number of pattern stitches needed to complete your garment, and off you go! Of course, you might have to change your final width measurement a little in order to accommodate the stitch multiple for your particular stitch pattern. Knitwear design and pattern drafting are more an art form than an exact science.

color PLAY

You can use schematic illustrations such as those found in this book as size guidelines for specific projects, or you can draw shapes of your own.

Knitting Techniques

Bobbles

Bobbles introduce surface texture to fabrics. Though time-consuming to knit, they add a bit of whimsy and are not at all difficult. To make a bobble, work several stitches into a single stitch, increasing the number of stitches in that area from 1 stitch to 3, 5, or more. Work several rows on these new stitches, turning the work after each successive row. Finally, decrease the stitches back to the original single stitch.

Cable Cast-On

This particular cast-on is my favorite cast-on technique: It's beautiful, quick, and easy to do. Plus, it's perfect when the first row worked is a right-side row.

Begin by making a slip knot on your knitting needle, then insert the tip of the right-hand needle knitwise into the loop that's sitting on the left-hand needle and knit a stitch (illustration 1) *but don't remove the original stitch from the left-hand needle*; instead, transfer the new stitch from the right-hand needle back to the left-hand one. One new stitch has been cast on.

[1]

For each successive stitch to be cast on, insert the tip of the right-hand needle *between* the first 2 stitches on the left-hand needle to knit a stitch (illustration 2).

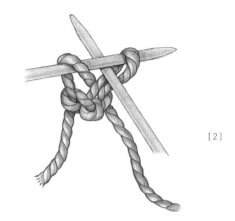

[2]

As before, do not remove the old stitch, but slip the new one back onto the left-hand needle; repeat until you have cast on the required number of stitches.

Fasten Off

To finish a piece of fabric securely once the knitting is completed, cut the yarn leaving at least a 6"/[15cm] tail, and fasten off by drawing the loose tail through the remaining stitch on the knitting needle. Later, this yarn tail can be used for seaming or else must be woven in (page 36).

K2tog Decrease

Here's the simplest kind of decrease, and the resulting stitch slants toward the right. Just insert your right-hand knitting needle into 2 stitches at once instead of 1 stitch and knit them together as 1 stitch (illustration 3).

[3]

Note: For a K3tog, use the same method to combine 3 stitches into 1 stitch.

Knit-On Cast-On

This cast-on technique is similar to the cable cast-on except new stitches are created by working directly into stitches rather than in between them. See page 46 for complete instruction.

Knitwise

Instructions will sometimes tell you to insert your knitting needle into a stitch knitwise. To do this, simply insert the tip of your right-hand needle into the indicated stitch as if you were about to knit that stitch—in other words, from left to right and *from front to back* (illustration 4).

[4]

If you're told to slip a stitch knitwise, insert the tip of your right-hand needle into the indicated stitch as if you're about to knit it and slide that stitch off of the left-hand needle and onto the right-hand one, allowing the stitch to sit on the right-hand needle with its left "leg" in the front. Usually, stitches are slipped knitwise during a decrease.

Make One Increase (M1, M1-L, or M1-R)

This method of increasing is the most invisible and perhaps the most useful one to have in your knitting repertoire. It can be made to slant toward the left *(abbreviated M1-L)* or toward the right *(abbreviated M1-R)*. If the slanting direction is not specified, use the increase that slants left. Used in combination, left- and right-slanting stitches can create beautiful, symmetrical sleeve increases.

To Make One slanting to the left (M1-L), use the left-hand needle to scoop up the horizontal strand that's hanging between the needles *from front to back*, and knit the strand *through its back loop*, twisting it to prevent a hole in your fabric (illustration 5).

[5]

To Make One slanting to the right (M1-R), use your left-hand needle to scoop up the horizontal strand that's hanging between the needles from back to front and knit the strand through its front loop, twisting it to prevent a hole in your fabric.

P2tog Decrease

This technique combines 2 purl stitches into 1 stitch, and it's usually worked on wrong-side rows; the resulting stitch slants toward the right on the right side of the fabric.

To do it, simply insert your right-hand needle into 2 stitches at once and purl them together as 1 stitch (illustration 6).

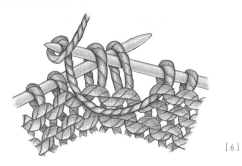

[6]

Note: For a P3tog, use the same method to combine 3 stitches into 1 stitch.

Purlwise

When instructed to insert your knitting needle into a stitch purlwise, simply insert the tip of your right-hand needle into the indicated stitch as if you were about to purl that stitch—in other words, from right to left and *from back to front* (illustration 7).

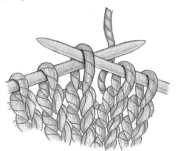

[7]

The convention in knitting is to always slip stitches purlwise unless told otherwise. When instructed to slip a stitch purlwise, insert the tip of your right-hand needle into the indicated stitch as if you're about to purl it and slide that stitch off of the left-hand needle and onto the right-hand one, allowing the stitch to sit on the right-hand needle with its right "leg" in the front.

S2KP2 Decrease

Here's a central double decrease that takes 3 stitches down to 1 stitch.

To do it, slip 2 stitches at once *knitwise* (illustration 8), knit the next stitch (illustration 9), then pass the 2 slipped stitches over the stitch you just knitted (illustration 10).

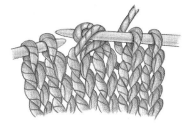

[8]

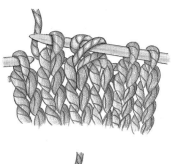

[9]

[10]

SSK Decrease

This decrease—known as "slip, slip, knit"—slants toward the left. It requires two steps to complete.

First slip 2 stitches *knitwise*, one at a time from the left-hand needle onto the right-hand one (illustration 11).

Then insert the tip of the left-hand needle into the fronts of these 2 stitches and knit them together from this position (illustration 12).

Then insert the tip of the right-hand needle *through the back loops* of the 2 stitches (going into the second stitch first) and purl them together from this position (illustration 13).

[13]

Note: For an SSSP decrease, use the same method, but slip 3 stitches and then purl them together into 1 stitch.

Yarn Over Increase (yo)

This type of increase creates a decorative hole in knitted fabric and is most often used to make lace and other openwork patterns. It is done differently depending on whether the next stitch to be worked will be knitted or purled.

For a yarn over immediately before a knit stitch, bring the working yarn to the front, between the tips of the knitting needles. As you knit the next stitch, the yarn will go over the right-hand needle to create the extra stitch.

For a yarn over immediately before a purl stitch, the working yarn must be brought to the front, between the tips of the knitting needles, and then wrapped *completely around* the right-hand needle and back to the front.

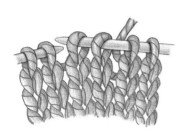

[11]

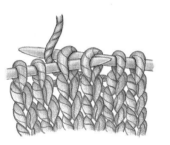

[12]

Note: For an SSSK decrease, use the same method, but slip 3 stitches and then knit them together into 1 stitch.

SSP Decrease

Here's a decrease that's most often used on wrong-side rows; the resulting stitch slants toward the left on the right side.

Slip the 1st and 2nd stitches *knitwise* one at a time from the left-hand needle onto the right-hand one. Then slip them back to the left-hand needle, keeping them twisted.

Finishing Techniques

Blocking

Prior to seaming your knitted pieces, take the time to block them into shape. You'll be surprised at how this simple process can improve the appearance of your projects and can tame even the most unruly stitches! To do it, follow the laundering instructions on the yarn label, then use rustless pins to shape the damp fabric to your desired measurements and allow it to dry. Or gently steam the pieces into shape by placing a damp cloth over them and then carefully wafting a hot steam iron just above the fabric. Don't actually touch the iron to the fabric or you'll risk flattening it.

Hiding Yarn Tails

Color knitting, by definition, involves lots of yarn ends. To make finishing your projects easier—and to make yourself a happier knitter—use the techniques discussed on page 36 to weave in the tails as you go as often as possible. For any yarn tails that remain at the end of a project, refer to page 37 for how to weave them in.

Mattress Stitch Seams

Here's the neatest seam imaginable for stockinette stitch and most knitted fabrics. Nearly invisible, it can be worked vertically or horizontally.

For a vertical seam: Lay your pieces flat, with the right sides of the fabric facing you, matching patterns and stripes, if applicable.

Thread a blunt-end yarn needle with your sewing yarn, then bring the needle up *from back to front* through the left-hand piece of fabric, going in 1 stitch from the edge, leaving a 6"/[15cm] tail.

Bring the yarn up and through the corresponding spot on the right-hand piece to secure the lower edges.

Insert the needle *from front to back* into the same spot on the left-hand piece where the needle emerged last time and bring it up through the corresponding place of the next row of knitting.

Insert the needle *from front to back* into the same spot on the right-hand piece where the needle emerged last time and bring it up through the corresponding place of the next row of knitting.

Repeat the last two steps until you've sewn approximately 2"/[5cm], then pull firmly on the sewing yarn to bring the pieces of the fabric together, allowing the 2 stitches on the edges of each piece to roll to the wrong side.

Continue this way until your seam is complete (illustration 14).

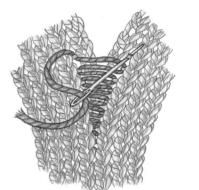

[14]

For a horizontal seam: Lay your pieces flat with the right sides of the fabric facing you and with the bound-off edges of the pieces together. Bring the needle up through the center of a stitch just below the bound-off edge on the lower piece of fabric, then insert it *from front to back* and from right to left around both legs of the corresponding stitch on the other piece of fabric. Bring the needle tip back down through the center of the same stitch where it first emerged.

Continue this way until your seam is complete (illustration 15).

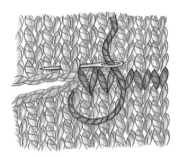

[15]

Invisible Seaming for Garter Stitch

Thread a blunt-tip yarn needle, and with the right sides of fabric next to each other and facing you on a flat surface, insert the needle into the top loop of the edge stitch (the ridge) of one piece of fabric and then into the bottom loop of the corresponding stitch (the ridge) on the other piece.

Continue this way until your seam is complete (illustration 16).

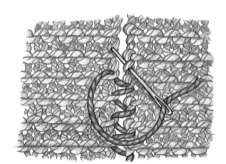

[16]

Sewing in a Zipper

Don't be afraid to add a zipper to a sweater! It's really quite easy to do. With the zipper closed and the right side of the garment pieces facing you, pin the zipper into place, keeping in mind that with hairier fabrics, it might be best to allow more of the teeth to show, so the fibers don't get caught in the zipper. Use contrasting sewing thread to baste the zipper into place (illustration 17).

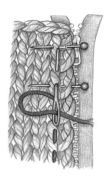

[17]

Remove the pins, and with matching sewing thread, use whipstitch to sew the tape to the wrong side (illustration 18). Finally, with the right side of the garment facing you, use backstitch to sew down the zipper tape neatly (illustration 19). Fold any excess zipper tape to the wrong side and tack it down.

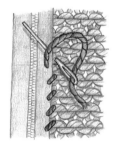

[18]

[19]

Sweater Assembly

Sweater pieces fit together like a jigsaw puzzle, with the type of armhole determining how the Front, Back, and Sleeves interlock. Refer to the illustrations below when assembling sweaters.

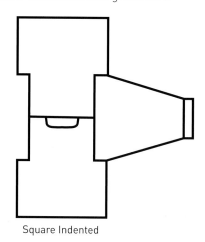

Square Indented

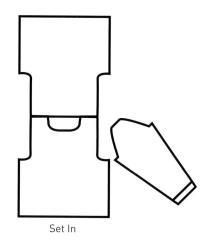

Set In

Yarn Choice and Substitution

Each project in this book was designed for a specific yarn. Different yarns possess their own characteristics, which will affect the way they appear and behave when knitted. In order to duplicate the projects exactly as photographed, I suggest that you use the designated yarns.

However, if you would like to make a yarn substitution, be sure to choose one of similar weight to the one called for in the pattern. Yarn sizes and weights are usually located on the label; but for an accurate test, knit a swatch of stockinette stitch pattern using the recommended needle size, making it at least 4"/[10cm] square.

Count the number of stitches in this 4"/[10cm] swatch and refer to the table below to determine the yarn's weight.

CYCA	1	2	3	4	5
Yarn Weight	Lace, Fingering, Sock	Sport	DK, Light Worsted	Worsted, Aran	Chunky
Avg. Knitted Gauge over 4" (10cm)	27–32 sts	23–26 sts	21–24 sts	16–20 sts	12–15 sts
Recommended Needle in US Size Range	1–3	3–5	5–7	7–9	9–11
Recommended Needle in Metric Size Range	2.25–3.25mm	3.25–3.75mm	3.75–4.5mm	4.5–5.5mm	5.5–8mm

Resources

I always recommend purchasing supplies at your local yarn shop. If there isn't one in your area, contact the appropriate wholesaler for more information.

Aurora Yarns
PO Box 3068
Moss Beach, CA 94038
(650) 728-2730
www.aurorayarns.net

Brown Sheep Company, Inc.
100662 County Road 16
Mitchell, NE 69357
(308) 635-2198 / (800) 826-9136
www.brownsheep.com

Cascade Yarns
1224 Andover Park E
Tukwila, WA 98188
(206) 574-0440
www.cascadeyarns.com

GGH
(see Muench Yarns)

JHB International, Inc.
1955 South Quince Street
Denver, CO 80231
(303) 751-8100 / (800) 525-9007
www.buttons.com

Judi & Co.
18 Gallatin Drive
Dix Hills, NY 11746
(631) 499-8480
www.judiandco.com

Knitcraft
215 North Main
Independence, MO 64050
(816) 461-1248
www.knitcraft.com

Louet North America
3425 Hands Road
Prescott, ON, Canada K0E 1T0
(613) 925-4502 / (800) 897-6444
www.louet.com

Muench Yarns
1323 Scott Street
Petaluma, CA 94954
(707) 763-9377 / (800) 733-9276
www.muenchyarns.com

Ornaghi Filati
(see Aurora Yarns)

Plymouth Yarn Company, Inc.
500 Lafayette Street
Bristol, PA 19007
(215) 788-0459
www.plymouthyarn.com

Trendsetter International
16745 Saticoy Street, Suite 101
Van Nuys, CA 91406
(818) 780-5497 / (800) 446-2425
www.trendsetteryarns.com

The Knitting Community

To meet other knitters and to learn more about the craft, contact the Knitting Guild Association. I currently sit on their Advisory Board and can attest to the educational value—and the pure, knitterly fun—of this group.

Knitting Guild Association
1100-H Brandywine Boulevard
Zanesville, OH 43701-7303
(740) 452-4541
E-mail: TKGA@TKGA.com
www.tkga.com

To attend workshops given by myself and others on educational, fun-filled cruises all over the world, contact:

Craft Cruises
1200 Western Ave #522
Seattle, WA 98101
(206) 579-1953
www.craftcruises.com

To meet other knitters online, visit:

www.ravelry.com

Acknowledgments

I am most grateful to the following knitters for knitting samples for this book: Carol Buchholz, Jen Chin, Corrina Ferguson, Gerry Futoran, Nancy Hand, Erica Hernandez, Tom Jensen, Cheryl Keeley, Betsy Mamo, Peggie Meyer, Joan Murphy, Veronica Ory, Dawn Penny, Kathy Redman, Marina Salume, Norma Jean Sternschein, Angie Tzoumakas, Vanessa Vine, and Lauren Waterfield.

A giant thank-you goes to Jocelyn Grayson for working behind the scenes with me. I could not have managed this project without you!

I'm grateful to Cascade Yarns Company for providing *tons* of its beautiful Cascade 220 yarn for nearly all of the swatches in the book. This yarn is fantastic: It is well priced, has great yardage per hank, feels wonderful to knit, and is available in nearly a gazillion colors. Many thanks, Jean and Shannon, for your generosity and support for this project.

Thank you, Peggy Wells and Brown Sheep Yarn Company, for sending all the yarn for Chapter 1. Brown Sheep Yarn Company's Naturespun Yarn comes in several different weights—and in a veritable kaleidoscope of colors, perfect for depicting the color wheel. Bonus point: It's American-made—in a family-owned mill in Nebraska.

Clearly, I've been fortunate to have been able to surround myself with the best folks in the business: my technical illustrator, Joni Coniglio, and my tech editor, Charlotte Quiggle. Your combined insight and experience made this book so much better than it would have been otherwise. Thank you. One of these days, we'll work on something a bit smaller and more manageable, I promise! <grin>

Index

In loving memory
of
Ada Leapman

MAY - - 2010

Copyright © 2010 by Melissa Leapman

All rights reserved.

Published in the United States by Potter Craft,
an imprint of the Crown Publishing Group, a division of Random House, Inc., New York.
www.crownpublishing.com
www.pottercraft.com

POTTER CRAFT and colophon is a registered trademark of Random House, Inc.

Library of Congress Cataloging-in-Publication Data
Leapman, Melissa.
Color knitting the easy way : essential techniques, perfect palettes, and fresh designs
using just one color at a time / by Melissa Leapman.—1st ed.
p.   cm.
Includes index.
ISBN 978-0-307-44942-9
1. Knitting. 2. Color in art. I. Title.
TT820.L386 2010
746.43'2—dc22   2009032312

Printed in China

Design by Kathleen Phelps
Fashion photography by Alexandra Grablewski
Flat fabric photography by Jacob Hand
Technical illustrations by Joni Coniglio
Charts and schematic illustrations by Melissa Leapman
Technical editing by Charlotte Quiggle

Thanks to the Craft Yarn Council of America (www.yarnstandards.com) for its
Standard Yarn Weight System chart, which appears on page 156.

10 9 8 7 6 5 4 3 2 1

First Edition